Advance P...

"Some days your mind and soul just crave encouraging sustenance. That's what Tom and Jared have put together here—a compilation to assure that you deserve to live your dreams and a nurturing step-by-step guidebook to show you how to get there."

— LAUREN MUSCARELLA, Founder, Trauma to Art:
Turning Grief into Creative Expression

"This book reinforces the power each one of us has inside of us. Unleashing this power leads to success ONLY if we decide to follow OUR personal dream. Only then can we come to a truly amazing place in our life. Those who choose to follow their dreams, despite sometimes difficult obstacles, experience amazing results! Tom and Jared bring to life thought provoking stories that leave us wondering—am I really following MY dream?"

— RICHARD J. MARKIEWICZ, Senior Professional Human
Resources; Certified Professional Empowerment Coach

"*One Door Closes* is a wonderfully inspirational and spiritually uplifting book that leaves the reader with gratitude and hope. It shows the power of positive thoughts and empowers you to take positive, directed steps to live the life you envision for yourself. A masterpiece!"

— DR. KAREN WAY, Holistic Chiropractic Physician

"*One Door Closes* is a testament to the power of the human spirit. Overcoming adversity continues to be the breeding ground of empowerment and the inspiration to pursue dreams. Tom and Jared have not only experienced this themselves, but they have assembled an amazing group of people with similar experiences. I highly recommend this book to anyone looking for inspiration and encouragement to never let their dreams die!"

— RICK MUHR, Co-Founder & Head Coach, The Marathon Coalition, Empowering Others Through Running

One
Door
Closes

Overcoming Adversity by Following Your Dreams

To Rachel -
your brother loves you!
Live into your dreams!
Tom Ingrassia
8/8/14

One Door Closes

Overcoming Adversity by Following Your Dreams

TOM INGRASSIA
JARED CHRUDIMSKY

MotivAct
publishing

ONE DOOR CLOSES
OVERCOMING ADVERSITY BY FOLLOWING
YOUR DREAMS

By Tom Ingrassia & Jared Chrudimsky
© 2013 MotivAct Group, LLC

ISBN 9781939288257
Library of Congress Control Number: 2013946913

Printed in the United States of America.

MotivAct
publishing

Published by MotivAct Publishing
An Imprint of Wyatt-MacKenzie

Dedication

Tom: To my wife, best friend and life partner, Barbara, who told me in 2001, "This is your dream, and I'll support you in any way I can." As Billy Dee Williams said to Diana Ross in "Mahogany," "Success is nothing without someone you love to share it with."

To my Mom and Dad, whom I miss every day. You taught me to be my own person and go my own way (right from age 5, when I insisted on picking out my own clothes for my first day of kindergarten!)—even when you didn't understand what I was doing. You were watching over me on April 15, 2013.

To Mary Wilson, my mentor, teacher and inspiration. You taught me to believe in my dreams—and to dream big. You opened a door for me.

Jared: To Kenzie, Jaxton, and Topher—my herd 'o children. You are my constant inspiration. I'm a lucky dad.

Acknowledgements

Tom: There are so many, many people who are responsible for this book! First and foremost, I thank God for the doors that have opened to me time after time on my journey—and for always sending just the right person into my life just when I need them most. It has been a long and winding road getting here—but this is THE dream!

A very heartfelt THANK YOU to each of the people who share their stories in these pages. Know that by sharing of yourselves so openly and selflessly, your messages of hope, healing and empowerment ARE making a difference in the lives of others.

Thank you, Jean Jesensky, for referring us to Nancy Cleary at Wyatt-MacKenzie Publishing—we couldn't have found a better or more supportive publisher. Thank you, Nancy!

Ken McDonnell, thank you for editing the chapters and for your encouragement, support, and the tears. Affirmation of the power in these pages.

Lynne McKenney Lydick and Tom Lydick, thank you for suggesting that we include Annette Rafferty in our book. Rob Donnan, thank you for referring us to Glenn Nazarian. Amy Mosher, thank you for connecting us with Reed Nixon.

Very early in my life—as you will read in the pages that follow—I fell in love with an incredible group of women—the 60s Girl Groups! It was their music that fueled my childhood dreams—dreams that are now reality. Imagine my profound delight when I found myself working for and with many of these women when I went into business for myself—Mary Wilson of The Supremes, Arlene Smith of The Chantels, Barbara Alston of The Crystals, June Monteiro of The Toys, Cal, Bertha, Norma and Milly of The Velvelettes. Each of you, in your own way, taught me valuable life lessons that I carry with me to this day. Your music continues to inspire me every day! And it powers me through those long runs. I also had the great pleasure of working with the late Carl Gardner of The Coasters on his autobiography, and with Dee Wallace. How lucky can you get??

I have a huge extended family—aunts, uncles, cousins all over the country and around the world. So many memories of happy times together—especially those summers at the Jersey Shore! So much of who I am today came through my family. And my nephews, nieces, grand-nephews and grand-nieces—I love being Uncle Tom (I just don't have a cabin!!). Good job raising some pretty neat kids, Joe & Bonnie!

Ulf Wahlberg, my Swedish LilleBror. Who knew when Barbara and I showed up on your doorstep in Stockholm on March 16, 1997—sight unseen—that we would become best friends within hours?!

Scott Lamlein, you appeared out of nowhere at a low point in my life, offered a hand of friendship, and opened yet another door for me. Thanks for sharing your great affirmations for the book.

David Barnard, we've been there for each other through thick and thin for almost forty years. You are my oldest friend. J

Last, but not least, thank you, Jared, for coming up with the amazing title for this book—it was the key that unlocked what had been roiling in my head for fifteen years! You embody the essence of what I have always thought true friendship is all about. Thank you for teaching me that indelible lesson!

Jared: First and foremost, thank you, Tom. You were the driving force behind getting this book out of our heads and into print. You motivate me every day. I'll always be sorry for abandoning you in Boston....

Thanks to my mom—Sue—and Kevin for being the most encouraging and loving parents. I know you weren't excited about me leaving college for massage school, but you were nothing but supportive. It took some time, but it wasn't the worst decision I've ever made.

Thanks to my dad, Paul, for teaching me so much about being who you are, not what people want you to be. I wish you were around to see how good your offspring are turning out. You would be proud.

Thanks, Uncle Ed, for teaching me work ethic. Darn kids nowadays don't wanta do nothin'.

Thanks, Kristin, for doing the lion's share of raising our amazing kids. They are going to make a mark on this world.

In no particular order, thanks, Pete and Sheila Rawson and Lynn and Joe and Linc and the whole Worcester Fitness team, all my roomies over the years who allowed me to keep my house, Shannon and Ari and everyone else who has done a massage at Revitalize, Paul Wasgatt, Marianne Allen Jeneski Brescia, Efay Imani, BNI, ACICS, and the whole UMass Worcester crew.

Thank you, Caroline, for calling me. I'm glad I handed you my card.

And James Chism—Miss you, buddy.

This acknowledgement thing is a lot of pressure—if I left you out, it's just because I didn't want you to see your name in print and get a big head about it! J

Table of Contents

PART ONE

*Inspirational Stories of Hope, Healing
and Empowerment*

CHAPTER ONE **Tom Ingrassia** *Learn From The Turtle* *1*

In 2001—at age 48 and just days before the 9/11 terrorist attacks, Tom left a successful, 25-year career in higher education to pursue his childhood dream of working in the entertainment industry.

CHAPTER TWO **Jared Chrudimsky** *Dreams Achieved Lead To More Dreams Dreamed* *15*

Picking up the pieces of his shattered life following a divorce, Jared re-discovered himself, building a successful career as a licensed massage therapist, teacher, writer and co-founder of an innovative motivational program.

CHAPTER THREE **Nancy Dube** *A Center of Influence* *29*

Breaking free from an abusive marriage, and building on her expertise as a human resource manager, Nancy took a leap of faith to form her own HR consulting company.

CHAPTER FOUR **Scott Erb & Donna Dufault** *What Are Your Gratefuls Today?* *35*

The dynamic duo behind the cameras at Erb Photography, Scott and Donna left behind years of broken dreams and dreams deferred for a life they are most grateful for.

CHAPTER FIVE **January Jones** *When A Door Opens, I Like To Walk Through It* *43*

Following the death of her first husband in a tragic helicopter accident, January found new love and a new life as a successful author and internet radio host.

P A R T   T W O
Living into MY Dreams

Introduction

What are **YOUR** aspirations and goals, **YOUR** hopes and dreams for **YOUR** life?

Do you believe in yourself ?

Do you believe that you **CAN** achieve your dreams?

Are you looking for a vehicle to break through those roadblocks and detours that may have sidetracked you on life's highway?

Do you have a "road map" to get from where you are now to where you truly want to be in life…with vision, courage, determination and passion?

In other words, are you living into your dreams?

In order to get what you want in life, you have to know what you want—and how to get it.

True dreams are hard to follow, and achieving them is not always easy. They don't just fall into your lap. You have to nurture them. You have to work hard to give them a chance to thrive. You have to persevere against what may seem like insurmountable obstacles and roadblocks. But if you truly believe in yourself and in your dreams—and if you are willing to take an honest look at yourself and commit to taking 100% responsibility for your life— then we guarantee that your dreams will come true.

And we know…you are sitting there, reading this and thinking, who are these guys and how are they going to help me?

We did not write this book to say, "Hey, look at us and all

the cool things we have done in our lives. Look at all these other really cool people we have assembled here."

Sure, we both have had some pretty amazing life experiences. But, we are not superheroes. We don't possess any superhuman powers. We are no different than you. We are just a couple of ordinary guys who have found the key to live into our dreams and to get the life we want! And so have the other people profiled in this book. We illustrate the fact that even the most ordinary people CAN achieve extraordinary things in life—if you believe in yourself, know what you want, and are willing to take the risks necessary to get it.

Each person profiled in this book has an amazing story that they are willing to share with you. Many are sharing their stories publicly for the first time. These are stories that demonstrate the importance of having the courage to change, of seizing the opportunities that are presented to you and making them your own—even if those opportunities do not seem perfect at first glance, and the importance of never giving up until you achieve your goals…no matter the roadblocks you encounter. Full speed ahead, emergency brake off—roadblocks and all. As the old saying goes, "when one door closes, a window opens." The key is recognizing the challenge of that closed door as an opportunity to open the window and look out onto a bright, new future. You CAN overcome those stubborn obstacles by living into your dreams.

Our goal with "One Door Closes" is to motivate you to achieve your heart's desire. This is a guidebook to help you clarify, set—and achieve!—your personal and professional goals. The book is divided into two sections. Part One features the stories of an amazing group of people who have overcome all manner of obstacles in their lives to achieve their dreams. You will read first-person accounts from Scherrie Payne, of The Supremes, and June Monteiro of 60s Girl Group, The Toys. The supreme Supreme, Mary Wilson, shares a very special message in the Epilogue of the book. But you will also read the stories of ordinary people, who have achieved the extraordinary—against all odds! Each person shares with you the wisdom they have learned on their journey—usually the hard way! Use this wisdom to your benefit.

Part Two of the book is your own, personal Dream Journal. It is important to check in with yourself periodically, as a blueprint for a more satisfied and productive life. You will find ten self-assessment tools—leverage them to help you discover your true purpose and then to develop the road map (action plan!) to get from where you are now to where you want to be in life. There are also blank pages for you to record your thoughts—your hopes and dreams, goals and aspirations. Take the time to really think about these assessments—and to answer them honestly. They are not easy. We will ask you to dig deep within yourself to identify what truly motivates you...and what is blocking you. In doing so, you will discover the incredible power that acknowledging and affirming your dreams will have in your life. That power is already there inside you. All you need do is unleash it.

Our holistic approach to personal and professional development has guided people from all walks of life to overcome those stubborn obstacles as they live into their dreams. And we are ready to guide you, too.

So, sit back, relax, and prepare to be inspired as we guide you on a fantastic journey into your future...your dreams!

Unlock your TRUE potential!

Fulfill your dreams!

Be inspired!

Jared and Tom

PART ONE

Inspirational Stories of Hope, Healing and Empowerment

C H A P T E R   1

Learn From the Turtle

Tom Ingrassia

Tom Ingrassia, president of The MotivAct Group LLC, is a motivational speaker, success coach, writer and musicologist. Re-inventing himself in 2001, after a successful, 25-year career in higher education administration, Tom is an in-demand speaker. He travels the country with the motivational programs, "Mental Massage®" and "Making A Difference Begins With YOU…So Live Into Your Dreams," as well as multimedia lecture programs that focus on the pop culture of the 1960s. He has worked with The Rock and Roll Hall of Fame and Museum, Vocal Group Hall of Fame, National Conference on Race and Ethnicity, Association for Continuing Higher Education, The Albany Institute of Art and History, The Long Island Museum, Hanover Theatre for the Performing Arts, and Worcester Art Museum. He has been married to Barbara Combes Ingrassia for 38 years.

Here is my story:

Music....That's all I ever wanted. Music and the chance. But, growing up, the music teacher and the band director said I wasn't good enough. That I didn't have any talent.

But I had a dream!

Music has always played a pivotal role in my life. My earliest recollections are of sitting next to my little portable record player, rocking back and forth, mesmerized by the magic coming out of the speaker (in those days, record players had only one, internal, speaker).

You see, that's all I ever wanted—music. And, through the music, the chance to make a difference in someone's life.

Growing up in the 1960s, I fell in love with show business. I wanted to be part of the glamour and glitter. And in the 1960s, there wasn't anyone more glamorous or glittery than The Supremes.

I grew up with The Supremes. Don't misunderstand. I wasn't raised in Detroit's Brewster Housing Projects, where The Supremes lived. And for sure The Supremes did not live in tiny Middletown, New York, my hometown! No, our cultural and physical neighborhoods were hundreds of miles and a world apart. But in 1964, Diana Ross, Mary Wilson, and Florence Ballard—the legendary Supremes—burst into the American musical consciousness just as I was becoming aware of the music playing on the radio.

In fact, I'll never forget that summer of 1964, because that is when my dream was born. I was lying on the beach in Sea Bright, New Jersey, when all of a sudden I heard the most exquisite sound coming out of my ever-present transistor radio. (Don't remember transistors? Google that, young 'uns. The transistor was the iPod of my generation!)

It was The Supremes' "Where Did Our Love Go?"

Now, for an 11 year old white bread boy totally caught up in the Beatlemania craze sweeping the country (I had my Beatles trading cards, Beatles lunchbox, all their records...all of which I later sold! I could kick myself now, because they are worth a fortune….), that softly sensual, repetitive beat and those cooing voices were irresistible. Let me tell you, I was in love—head over heels in love!—and my life changed forever that day. From that point on, I could literally trace my life through The Supremes' music. They provided the soundtrack to my life. The Beatles were out, The Supremes were in. I started collecting everything I could about the group—news articles, pictures, records, joined their fan club. I learned as much as I could about The Supremes—all of the Motown groups, in fact.

And then it happened…December 27, 1964. I was watching "The Ed Sullivan Show," as we all did on Sunday nights in the 60s, and there they were. These three goddesses whom I idolized were right there in my living room. And they were singing just to me! I remember as clearly as if it happened yesterday, turning to my mother and saying, "I'm gonna meet them some day."

Remember, I'm 11-years old and living in a small town in upstate New York. What did I know about meeting celebrities? But something inside my soul moved as I watched that performance. And that set the course for the rest of my life. Even at that age, I knew there was a plan for my life. Looking back now, I realize that I was fortunate to find my passion so early in life.

Fast forward to the 1970s. My love of music had grown. I was a student at the State University of New York at Geneseo, studying history. I learned as much as I could about the history of popular music. By that time, my dream was to be a writer. So I wrote an article about The Supremes. I submitted it to magazine after magazine…and I got rejection slip after rejection slip. Just as I was about to give up, the editor for a now-defunct magazine called.

"Get us an interview with The Supremes, and we'll publish your article."

"Sure," I said, "I can do that!"

Then I hung up the phone and said to myself, "You can't do that! You're just a 19 year-old college kid. How are YOU going to score an interview with the world's most popular female group?"

Coincidentally (although I firmly believe that NOTHING ever happens by coincidence), about two weeks later, The Supremes were performing at the West Point Military Academy—near where I lived. I screwed up all my courage, went to the show, and sent a note backstage, explaining that I was a writer (I was brash even at that age!), and wanted to do an interview. Out comes this burly bodyguard. My knees were knocking, because I was sure he was going to throw me out. They probably thought I was a stalker! Instead, he handed me a slip of paper, and when I opened it, it read:

"Come backstage after the show, Tom, and I'll give you that interview. I'm looking forward to meeting you." And it was signed "Mary Wilson."

That interview became the first of almost 30 articles that I have published over the years (including in publications like *Billboard, Goldmine, San Francisco Hot Ticket, Wisdom, and Worcester Business Journal*). I was on my way! It had been less than eight years since that little boy said to his mother, "I'm gonna meet them some day...."

Still, I didn't really believe that this dream of mine was very practical. I mean, "normal" people don't leave the safety and security of a "normal" life for the entertainment world. Or do they?? So, I followed a fairly traditional career path—college, graduate school, marriage, a house. I spent the next 25 years working in higher education administration. I rose through the ranks, ultimately achieving the position of Assistant Dean at the Graduate School of Management at Clark University, in Worcester, Massachusetts. About as far as you can get from show business, right? Besides, I had already fulfilled my dream, hadn't I? After all, I had published an article and met The Supremes. What more was there?

So, while I never allowed my dream to fully die, I boxed it up and shoved it way to the back of the top shelf in a closet, with the rest of my memorabilia.

But then the calls from Mary Wilson started coming. "Tom, I'm working on my autobiography and need some research done. Can you help me? Can I borrow some photos from your collection?" And, "I want to start doing lectures about my life and experiences. Can you help me with the script? And, you work with colleges—maybe you can get me a few gigs?" Even though I was working full time at the University, every time those calls came, I said, "Sure, I can do that for you!"

And then it happened. Early in 2001, Mary Wilson was performing in Boston for two weeks in the musical "Leader of the Pack" at the Shubert Theater. She asked me to come to the theater every night to sell her merchandise in the lobby. I would get up at 5 every morning, do my university work until noon. Then I'd drive to Boston, work with Mary during the afternoon, and then head for the theater at night to sell her CDs, photos and other merchandise. After the show, the cast would go back to their hotel for a drink. Then I'd drive home, get to bed at 2 AM, get up at 5 and do it all over again. Some nights, I honestly do not know how I got home. At the end of those two weeks, though, I said, "WOW! I love this!"

One day, as we were walking down Newbury Street in Boston, Mary said to me, "I want to expand my merchandise business. I have so many creative ideas. You have business background. Would you be interested in managing the business with me?"

This was my golden opportunity—a dream beyond any other. And I wasn't about to let slip from my grasp. But…I didn't give up my university job…just yet. I was still too afraid of the future to give up that security. So, along with my wife, Barbara, I managed Supreme Legacy™ on the side.

That August, Mary said, "I'm going out on the road with 'Sophisticated Ladies' for the next six months, and I need someone with me full-time to handle the merchandise and help take care of things." And she turned to my wife and said, "Barb, would you be interested?"

This was a great honor for Barbara. But it was a wake up call and life lesson for me. This was MY dream. It was MY gig. And here it was being offered to someone else. I was...well, let's just say I was a tad annoyed.

But, you see, I had been too afraid to let anyone know what I REALLY wanted. Now I realized that I had to step forward and say what I wanted and what skills I brought to the table.

Barbara graciously declined Mary's offer...and gave me a healthy shove forward. And I jumped up and said, "Take me! Take me!!!!"

The next day, I submitted my resignation to the university. That little boy's dream had finally come true.

The "Sophisticated Ladies" tour was scheduled to begin in Atlantic City on September 16, 2001, and had been booked into theaters across the country for six months. Six months in Europe was to follow. Well, we all know the devastation that happened in New York City and elsewhere on September 11, 2001, and the chaos into which the entire world was plunged. Cast members couldn't fly in for rehearsals. Theaters were calling to cancel engagements. The world, the tour—and my life—were in shambles. That little boy in me grew up real fast! What was I going to do? I had left the security of my university job to pursue my dream—and now that dream seemed shattered. That's when I heard a little boy's voice somewhere deep inside me say, "You didn't come this far to fail now."

And that's when things REALLY started to happen. Mary called and said, "I have to keep my office running. Will you come to New York and be my office manager and help me get some projects off the ground? I can't pay your full salary right now, but I'll make it to you as soon as things turn around." That's exactly what I did, spending five days a week in post-9/11 New York City, working with Mary. And I did some pretty amazing things during that time—working with the Rock and Roll Hall of Fame (an unveiling ceremony and gala jam session for a series of Legendary

Girl Groups Commemorative Stamps, and the launch of The Mary Wilson Supremes Gown Collection), Vocal Group Hall of Fame, the Lyndon Johnson Presidential Library (Life in the Swingin' 60s), and two of those wonderful PBS concert specials we all watch during pledge month (where I had the opportunity to share an elevator with Aretha Franklin!).

I am most proud of the role I played in coordinating the Legendary Girl Groups Stamp Ceremony. Mary had been working on this project for a while with the International Philatelic Society, which had contracted with two countries in Africa and three Caribbean nations to issue postage stamps with the images of 12 of the legendary Girl Groups of the 1950s and '60s—The Chantels, The Cookies, The Angels, The Shirelles, Patti LaBelle and the Blubelles, The Dixie Cups, The Ronettes, The Crystals, The Marvelettes, Martha Reeves and The Vandellas, The Velvelettes, and The Supremes. On August 22, 2002, we assembled 33 original members of those 12 groups—the first time in history that all these women shared the same stage, and the first time in decades that some group members had seen each other and sung together. It was a day of healing and hope! "Entertainment Tonight" was there to film the event, the *Cleveland Plain Dealer* provided front page coverage. 1200 fans showed up—the largest event to date at the Museum. Following the unveiling of the stamps, there was a huge jam session on stage, featuring all of the legendary ladies. The "meet and greet" afterwards was so mobbed with fans that the Museum had to stay open for an hour past its usual closing time. I had been so busy coordinating all the details of the event (hotel rooms, food, transportation, etc., for the ladies), that it was only after the event that I realized that I had had a hand in creating a chapter in music history!

~∘~

As a result of meeting and working with all those singers, my phone started to ring. First, Barbara Alston, of The Crystals called, "I need someone to help me write my autobiography. Are you interested?" I am pleased to say that Barbara's autobiography, *There's No Other*, was published by AuthorHouse in 2007.

That project led to a call from Veta Gardner, wife of legendary Coasters founding member, the late Carl Gardner, asking me to serve as editor for his autobiography, *Yakety-Yak, I Fought Back*, also published in 2007.

And then, the legendary Arlene Smith, lead singer of The Chantels and writer of their biggest hit, "Maybe," called: "I am looking for a concert manager. Will you work with me?"

Dee Wallace, the actress most famous for her role as the mother in "ET," called, "Tom, we met several months ago at an event you attended with Mary Wilson. I like the way you work with her. Are you interested in managing my merchandise and lecture dates, too?"

I also worked briefly with another of the Motown Girl Groups, The Velvelettes (including landing them a gig during Super Bowl weekend in Detroit several years ago), and June Monteiro of The Toys.

Not only did I have my dream back—I now had a full-fledged entertainment management agency, working with the very artists I had grown up listening to and idolizing. Talk about a dream come true! And it had only taken me 38 years to get there.

You see, I always knew what my dream was. I knew what I wanted. But I let my own self-doubts and the naysayers hold me back for decades. What if people laughed at me? What if I failed? What would I say when people said, "I knew you couldn't do it." I didn't believe enough in myself or my dreams to take a stand. So I played it safe, ignoring the messages I was receiving from the Universe about my life purpose.

I had gone through most of my life feeling that I really didn't have much of anything to offer to anyone. That I was a fraud. Taking to heart what the music teachers and band director told me as a child—that I didn't have any talent. That I wasn't good enough.

But I discovered that I DO have talent—maybe not performing talent, but management talent. I AM a person of worth!

People who know me think that I've always had my act together. That was the public mask I always wore. Well, you are about to find out that nothing could be further from the truth. One of my nagging fears had always been how would I handle the "dark times" if they came? For most of my life, things came easily to me. I never really had to struggle. Could I survive the challenges? This new life I was living was challenging. I loved it! But, my courage, strength and confidence were severely tested in 2005, as I watched my life unravel. From out of nowhere, my whole world fell apart.

I saw the warning signs early in the year...and chose to ignore them, as we do so often. Someone I trusted stepped on my dream and betrayed my trust. Right before my eyes, that dream turned to dust. I understood for the first time that the entertainment industry isn't all sweetness and light, and that there is always someone ready to knock you off your perch.

Still, I kept hanging on, trying desperately to work it out. Until finally I realized that I had to walk away from my dream. THAT was the hardest life lesson of all. How was I going to give up my dream? If I stayed, though, I risked losing my dignity and self-respect. I had already lost much of my personal savings, which I had invested into the business. I had just $300 left in my savings account. Thank God my wife, Barbara, had a stable job that provided our health insurance. Here I was, 51 years old, and feeling like that little boy again—I wasn't good enough. A handful of empty promises was all I had left. And I realized it was, indeed, time to let go and move on. I had to find a way to get my life back on track. I had to find a way to survive!

My dream had become a nightmare. I had always told myself that if the dream ended, I could live with that. I was only fooling myself. I hit rock bottom—adrift in a boat so filled with the shards of my shattered dream that I thought I might never make it back to solid ground. I grasped as I watched my dream drift further away. All the while thinking to myself, "I don't want to lose this dream. It's all I ever wanted. If I lose this dream, I don't know what I'm going to do. Please, God, don't let me lose this dream. Where do I go from here?" And that's when I heard that little boy's voice again, somewhere deep inside me, say, "This is just the end of Chapter One, Tom. You are the only one who can write your story. Don't let someone else define your dream for you. The rest of your story has yet to be written. Turn the page and write your own story."

It was the best thing that ever happened to me…

A few weeks later, my phone rang again. It was a classical musician I'd met a few weeks earlier. I didn't really know him—and this rock and roll baby certainly knew NOTHING about classical music. But I knew enough to realize that he was a truly gifted musician. He said, "I understand you work in the entertainment industry. Can we have lunch some time? I'd like to pick your brain about re-launching my concert career." Now, I'm not used to getting answers to prayer quite that quickly. But that was fine with me—hey, it was a free lunch. What did I have to lose? Although I felt he would find pretty slim pickings in this brain.

By the end of that lunch, I had my answer. This musician—Scott Lamlein—who really knew nothing about me—asked me to be his manager. I responded, "But I don't know anything about the classical music world." And Scott replied, "Well, I don't know anything about management. Let's teach each other." And that's when I realized that this was the bridge that was going to take me into the next chapter of my life. By trusting in my abilities—sight unseen—at a time when I felt utterly devastated and desperately needed someone to believe in me—he opened a whole new world to me, one that I might not have discovered on my own. I realized for the first time that I had been blinded by loyalty to all that was wrong. I had been seduced by the trappings of my success—

London and Stockholm, Los Angeles and Las Vegas, the Ritz Carlton, limousines, champagne and cognac. And that wasn't why I had gotten into this business…well…maybe just a little! For so many years, though, the answer was right there in front of me, but I didn't see it. I was the only one in control of my own destiny. I just needed to believe in myself the way that others had always believed in me—AND to be open to new ideas. Now, I was no longer chained to yesterday. I was finally free to find my own destiny—no longer letting anyone else define my dream for me. And the next chapter of my life began

Starting in 2006—and prompted by some of my former colleagues in higher education—I decided to share what I had learned—sometimes the hard way—about the power of following your dreams, inspiring others to live into their dreams the way I have lived into mine. I developed my first motivational lecture and workshop, "Making A Difference Begins With YOU…So Live Into Your Dreams!" incorporating guided visioning with self-motivational tips and techniques, and took it on the road. I offered the program for professional groups, college students, job seekers. I was an instant hit, and I became an in-demand speaker!

In 2008, I met Jared Chrudimsky through a networking group. We made an immediate connection, knowing that we had been brought together for a purpose, but not yet understanding what that purpose was. Over the next couple of years, we became best friends and running buddies. (Running is a whole other chapter of my life. Maybe I'll share THAT story with you later in this book!) In late 2010, Jared and I were coincidentally scheduled to make presentations to our networking group on the same day—but remember that I firmly believe that nothing ever happens by coincidence. There was a reason we were scheduled for the same day. During an early morning run a couple of weeks before our presentations, Jared said, "I always do a massage demonstration for my presentation. I'd like to try something different this time. How about if you do your guided visioning exercise with the group, and while you do I'll give everyone a brief neck and shoulder massage?"

"Huh?" I said! I honestly could not see how that would work. Besides, I was used to working alone!

But the more I thought about it, the more sense it made. I realized that we had something very powerful there. On our next run, I said to Jared, "Let's go for it—and if we get a good response from the group, then we need to develop this idea and take it on the road."

The response from the 60 people in the group that morning was overwhelming. And on December 4, 2010, our new workshop, "Mental Massage" was born. By early January of 2011, we had developed a full-fledged program, developed promotional materials, set up a website. And we offered our first program in early February—for employees at a financial services company. Jared and I finally realized the purpose for our coming together—and we have never looked back! We each maintain our own businesses, and we have this marvelous new business partnership, The MotivAct Group, through which we offer a full menu of holistic personal and professional development programs.

Today, because I now believe in myself and in my dreams, my life has changed dramatically. I travel all over the country with my motivational programs, as well as lecture programs about the interaction between music, culture and society in the 1960s. Me. That little boy with a little boy's dreams. Doing the work I was born to do! Better late than never. I still believe in chasing dreams.

You see, all I ever wanted was the music. And the chance. The chance to make a difference in someone's life. Because I know that if I can make a difference in even just one person's life, then I will have changed the world for the better. I will have made a difference. And it all started with the music coming out of that little transistor radio in the summer of 1964. You never know where you will find your inspiration. If I had it to do all over again, I wouldn't change a thing. Even those dark days taught me perhaps the greatest life lesson of all—I DO have the strength and the courage—and the faith—to survive—and to thrive.

Almost a half century ago (!!!), I had what many said was an Impossible Dream. But, it's just like in the "Wizard of Oz"—when you know your mind, when you know your heart, when you know your courage…when you know yourself—and when you have the courage to take the risk—you can achieve your heart's desire.

It is no longer important whether or not I please others. My life speaks for itself. My triumphs have come in ways that are significant to me. I no longer fear where the road is leading. I still know the power of music. And I still believe in dreams coming true!

Vincent Van Gogh said, "I dream my painting, then I paint my dream." In order to get what you want in life, you have to know what you want. You have to be able to see the opportunities that are right in front of you.

So to those of you reading this who are still searching for your dream, don't give up. Maybe you don't have all the answers right now. Maybe it feels like to much of a quest. To you I say, channel the inspiration I felt as an 11 year old boy, feeling something stir inside me as I watched the images on my television screen. Take the chance. Don't ever let anyone say that you didn't try. If there is something you have always wanted to do—DO IT! Step out on faith—and I mean deep water faith! What's the worst that can happen? If it doesn't work out exactly as planned… maybe there's a different, bigger plan for you.

We are continually presented with great opportunities disguised as great problems. I know that first-hand. Opportunities may not always be perfect. But if you don't take them—and make them your own—you may never have a second chance.

Don't ever stop reaching for the top, for your dreams. Because you know what? There's plenty of room at the top of the heap—it's the bottom of the pile that is full.

Have the courage to follow your heart. I guarantee that you WILL find your dream in that place where your mind meets your heart and your soul.

Learn from the turtle. It only makes progress when it sticks its neck out....

CHAPTER 2

Dreams Achieved Lead To More Dreams Dreamed

Jared Chrudimsky

Jared Chrudimsky is the owner of Revitalize Massage Therapy, in Worcester and Holden, Massachusetts. He is a six-time winner of *Worcester Magazine*'s "Best Massage Therapist" award, and a two-time winner of *The Landmark*'s "Best Massage Therapist" award. In 2013, he was named as one of *Worcester Business Journal*'s "Forty Under Forty" up-and-coming business leaders. From 2004 to 2010, Jared was an instructor and director of the massage therapy program at Salter College, in West Boylston, Massachusetts. As an independent contractor with the Accrediting Council of Independent Colleges and Schools, Jared evaluates massage therapy programs around the country for accreditation. Jared also serves as vice president of The MotivAct Group LLC.

Here is my story:

In 2004, my wife handed me her wedding ring and told me she wanted a divorce. This time, she meant it. Our relationship had been rocky for a long time. It was the happy memories, the fear of failure, and our kids that kept us together up to that point. For the next year and a half, I bounced between being miserable and depressed.

When I found out that Kristin was dating, it was like a dagger in my heart. When she started seeing an ex-boyfriend, whom she had previously assured me she had no romantic interest in, my heart cracked even deeper. So, when she sidled up all close to me one day and asked how I felt about moving from Massachusetts to San Diego—where she had been accepted to law school and had found a new job—I felt a strange elation. This could be the chance to rekindle our relationship.

Our oldest child, Kenzie, had been born in Minnesota. Jaxton was born in Atlanta. Our youngest, Topher, had just been born in Massachusetts. We could continue the trend of birthing new offspring in a new state! In August of 2005, Kristin packed up the kids and migrated west. I stayed behind to clean up loose ends— finding a new massage therapist for my clients, selling our house, closing up our bank accounts.

Because the moving company wouldn't haul it, I agreed to drive Kristin's car out to California, setting off a couple of days after they left. I had always loved road trips, and although I would be doing this road trip in a time frame that wouldn't allow for much sight-seeing, I was excited to be doing something that I loved. The trip turned into an exercise in endurance, a true test of my physical endurance and my tolerance of others.

I had posted an ad on craigslist, looking to do a ride share. I was honestly and naively hoping to find a fun road trip mate, someone who would share the driving duties and fuel costs, and help pass the time with spirited conversation. A couple of folks answered the ad, but no one wanted to traverse the country in three days. The guy who finally committed disappeared the day before I was to leave. It was probably just as well that it didn't work out. He emailed me a few months later and apologized— he'd been in the clink. I didn't ask for elaboration.

The only other taker was a woman in Shrewsbury, near Worcester where I lived. She and her boyfriend had just broken up, and she was moving back to Indianapolis to live with her family. That was just about exactly one third of the way to San Diego—or fourteen hours, according to the AAA Triptik. Better than nothing, I thought, and who knows, maybe she would be a cutie, or fun to talk to and full of interesting stories.

She turned out to be none of the above. I parked the car outside her apartment building at 10:00 on a Thursday night. She emerged after a few minutes, and lumbered toward the car, with a little Pekinese dog in tow. We made our introductions, and I loaded her luggage into my little Volvo S40. I opened the door for her and—for lack of a better term—she wedged herself into the front seat, with the dog sitting on her stomach. I climbed into the driver's seat, only to discover that with her ample girth, she had also taken up the center console and my armrest. We were in a Volvo, but not one of the spacious station wagons of yesterday. This was a sporty little coupe. It was going to be tight all the way.

The next discovery came within half a block. This poor woman explained that she had just done a thorough cleaning of her apartment before moving out. She was sweating out all sorts of acrid odors. It reminded me of a "Seinfeld" episode where a valet parks Jerry's car and it becomes impregnated with a horrific, irremovable odor. Even though it was a brisk evening, I cracked the window—afraid of leaving Kristin with an everlasting olfactory memory of her husband's road trip. "Oh, and by the way," she said, "I don't have my driver's license."

This was before everyone had iPods, so I put my travel buddy on CD changing duty. She wanted all country music, but unfortunately for her, I had nothing beyond maybe The Statler Brothers' "Flowers on the Wall," from the "Reservoir Dogs" soundtrack.

We got along pretty well for the first four hours. Her little fur ball was well behaved, perched atop her tummy. We stopped for gas and bladder relief at 2 am in upstate New York. I picked up an energy drink and some nosh to keep me going. She got two hamburgers from Micky D's—one for her and one for her doggy. Not what I'd feed a dog, but maybe that's one reason I am animal free!

I had decided hours before that I was not going to be crashing at a hotel that night. Just forge ahead. The next incident solidified that idea. I had noticed throughout the ride that when I handed her a CD to switch to, her hand would brush mine more than was necessary. I thought it was a body control issue, or hand-off accident. I was being nice and cordial (my Mom taught me manners!), but there was no way I was sending out romantic vibes.

The next song pumping out of the speakers was one of my favorite Lit songs, "Miserable." As the refrain was playing—"She makes me come. She makes me complete. She makes me completely miserable", her meaty hand rose from her belly, landed on my right thigh, and gave a squeeze. I almost burst out laughing. It fit so perfectly with the situation—all the sex talk about her ex-boyfriend, the hand brushing, the awakeness at 2 am. I handed her hand back to her and burbled something about still loving my ex-wife. I didn't want to hurt her feelings, but I didn't want to lead her on.

We made amazing time the rest of the way to Indy. I don't remember Pennsylvania. The dog started getting restless and shedding in Ohio. My potential amour bought me a meat stick as a thank you gift at our final fuel stop. I had her at the Greyhound station six hours before her family expected her. I stopped at the first rest stop outside of Indy and passed out for a couple of hours.

The rest of the trip went without a hitch, and I discovered something that I didn't expect. I liked traveling alone. I made all the decisions. No one had to approve of anything first. I stopped at the Meramec Caves in Stanton, Missouri, later that afternoon. They were closing for the day, but agreed to give me a last, solo tour of the day. It was beautiful and interesting, and the perfect reset to my road trip. I covered a whole lot more road that night, finally tipping back the seat and sleeping in the car in a filling station parking lot who knows where.

The rest of the way, I explored what is left of Route 66 (not much!), drove through the Petrified Forest in Arizona, and slurped down a date shake in Dateland, Arizona. I decided to spend one short night at a hotel. The next one I came across was the Space Age Lodge, in Gila Bend, Arizona. It was a super cool UFO-themed hotel straight out of the sixties. All told, my adventure lasted fifty-six hours. Mostly by myself. With a great story to tell.

It was around that time that I started feeling like it was going to be okay. I had spent six years with a woman from whom I was deriving all my happiness. If we weren't together, nothing was good. If we weren't together, I failed. Don't get me wrong, it was not as if a switch had flipped. I still had to get used to my kids living across the country from me. I still thought Kristin and I should and would get together. But a seed was planted. A new philosophy was growing. Good things can come from bad. Divorce is not the end of the world. You can find positives in any situation.

When I tell people my little road trip story, they usually say, "That sounds like a terrible trip! You'll probably never use craigslist and meet up with a stranger again." I have to completely disagree. It was a great trip that turned into a great story. And my favorite part was the part I did by myself. I want stories. I want things to happen. I want to make adjustments, to overcome adversity, to adapt. I want to see the bright side.

My kids live in San Diego. I live in Massachusetts. For those of you who are geographically challenged, that's nearly 3000 miles apart. My move to San Diego never happened. A couple of offers on the house fell through, followed by the market plummeting and the mortgage being under water. All the while, I was meeting new friends and building my business and connections—and getting used to visiting the kiddos and talking with them on the phone. In eight years, I have been out to see them a hundred times. I go to San Diego every month. Does it cost a lot of money? Of course. But when you want to make something happen, you make it a priority. I had to become travel-savvy in a hurry, and I have found ways to make it work. All the credit cards with the highest amount of miles are in my wallet. One airline gets most of my business because airline loyalty leads to more free miles, upgrades, free checked bags, shorter check-in queues, and special phone lines. It makes travel much more than just endurable—it is actually pleasurable and convenient.

I cut back on unnecessary luxuries in my life. My car is used and kind of old, but reliable and paid for. I strive to put good energy out into the Universe, and keep my mind and eyes open to receive the karma back.

And it keeps coming back. Once I stopped feeling sorry for myself, stopped blaming others for my misfortunes, and opened my mind to the good the cosmos want me to have, I see it and expect it everywhere.

In September, 2006, I was teaching massage courses at Salter College in Worcester. The director of the program, Dan DiMezza, had been invited on a couple of trips around the country to evaluate massage programs for the Accrediting Council of Independent Colleges and Schools (ACICS). When he described what that entailed, it sounded a little tedious, but evaluators receive a small stipend, plus all food, hotel and flight expenses are reimbursed.

One of my dreams had always been to be able to travel for work. Years ago, when I first got married, I was working for Wells Fargo in Minneapolis. I took a promotion within the company, and they sent me to Roseville, California, for two weeks of training. I loved the food, the hotel, the flight, the rental car, and meeting new people. I was able to visit Sacramento and the site of the first California gold rush in my limited free time. It was great! This experience and the cross country road trip described above proved to me that traveling alone could be fun and enlightening. If only I could have a job where I got to do more of that....

So, when, in September of 2006, Dan called me on Monday to say that a massage therapist evaluator had backed out of the next ACICS trip, and asked if I could be in New Jersey Tuesday night to take her place, I pushed down my terror of doing something completely unknown and said, "Of course I'll be there!"

I was trained on site, picked up the work quickly, and within a couple of years, I was being invited on as many site visits as the agency allowed. I accepted anything they would throw at me. The Dirty Jers. Bumblefudge, Missouri. Nowhere, Utah. I didn't care. Send me anywhere. I love traveling! I met amazing people who showed me fossils in the banks of the Ohio River in Louisville, Kentucky, by the light of a brilliant moon. People I'll never forget in Augusta, Georgia (I never would have guessed she was a transvestite...). Unexpected romances in Texas, California, and Wisconsin. My airline miles built up, allowing me to see my kids for free once in a while. The rare evaluations in and around San Diego, or the visits on both sides of a weekend, which allowed me to fit in a visit with the kids into my schedule. All of a sudden, visiting the kiddos was much less of a financial burden. Things were going great!

Meanwhile, I had a couple of spots of bad luck. For five years, I had been doing chair massages on Fridays for employees at Masterman's Safety and Industrial Supply, in Auburn, Massachusetts. It was a sweet gig that brought in a couple hundred bucks a week, plus some nice benefits—like free lunches and barbeques, and a big ol' holiday party. The owner, Ben Masterman, would often surprise us with gift certificates to local restaurants, a semi-subsidized trip to Las Vegas, and Christmas gifts like a leather jacket (that I still wear), and a digital camera and printer when he found out I didn't have one and wanted to take more pictures of my children. The only stipulation being that I show off the pictures.

I loved that job, the employees and the extra income. But, in February of 2009 I was informed that due to the tanking economy, some benefits were being cut, starting with the free massages. Masterman's gave me five weeks of severance—one week for each year I'd been there—and wished me luck. I was at a bit of a loss. I had a house payment and all the other regular bills—and child support, which my ex-wife was not willing to reduce. My own massage business, Revitalize Massage Therapy, was still in its infancy, still being run out of my house. I had a small, but steady, massage clientele at Worcester Fitness, and was teaching part-time at Salter. The ACICS job was great, but didn't pay especially well, and could be very unreliable in terms of volume of work.

In the midst of trying to recoup my losses and regroup, an old friend and my marketing guru at Vision Advertising, Laura Briere, called me out of the blue. She asked if I would like to go with her to a Business Network International (BNI) meeting, where she was a member. It was just down the road from my house, at 6:45 am. She said it would be a great way to do some networking, meet other small business people, and possibly drum up some new business. What else did I have to do on Friday morning? I thought, "Why not? What have I got to lose?"

It turned out to be quite a fateful decision. The meeting was very high energy, and I learned very quickly how useful this networking format could be for my (until now) slowly growing business. And outside of the potential business benefits, I met many great people who became friends, colleagues, and close peers.

Another significant event presented itself at about the same time. I had been doing massage out of my house since my family had moved away. I had set up my son Topher's, room as a massage room and saw a couple of clients a week—not a ton, but it supplemented my other income. It was not ideal, in that there were a few strange men that I gave massages to whom I would have preferred NOT know where I lived. And, I knew I was missing out on female clients, who felt skeptical about getting a massage from a guy they didn't know in his house. I couldn't find fault with that. It is a valid concern.

I had discussed these issues with a client of mine, and one day he asked if I was interested in expanding Revitalize and maybe renting a place in Worcester to do massages outside my home. He owned the building and would be willing to rent me a room there. It was a big room, next door to a hair stylist salon, on a busy street (but not overly so) with high visability. He said he would be happy to give me a break on the rent, since he knew I was just starting out, and he had faith in my skills. My first thought was to be responsible and turn it down. But, the more I pondered it, the more I decided that this was my logical next step, and the opportunity had been plopped right in front of me.

With this new location and the new contacts I was making, business started to trend upward even in a down economy. Within a few months, I was starting to cover the new rent with new business. I won a Best of Worcester award in a local magazine. Word of mouth was bringing new clients. I started building relationships with BNI folks, and began a friendship with Tom Ingrassia.

At first, he started coming to me for massages. Every month, then every two week, then almost every week he would get a massage and we would talk. We got to know each other and became good friends. We learned about each others' goals and aspirations, our passions and interests. A few times, he asked me about running, since he knew it was something I liked to do and wondered if it was something he might be capable of. I'm never one to discourage, so I said, "of course you can do it!" A few months passed and we continued to talk about it. Then, one morning, I ran from my house to his house and we did a relaxed two miler. I thought he was going to need medical attention with all of that huffing and wheezing! It didn't take long, though, before that 57 year old man was running three miles. Then five miles. Then ten miles. Then a half marathon, a marathon, and a twenty-four hour ultra marathon! I'm skipping ahead, though. That's his story to tell. His dreams became reality. And it was during those early morning hours of training that I discovered more about me and what I also wanted to accomplish. Mental Massage™ and The MotivAct Group were born out of those runs. This book was conceived on those miles of pavement. Dreams achieved lead to more dreams dreamed.

While Mental Massage™ and MotivAct were still being cultivated, I was continuing to teach part time at Salter. My new massage studio space was secure. BNI was bringing in new business and giving me a feeling of camaraderie with other self-employed entrepreneurs like myself. Things had turned around and were headed in the right direction again.

Then the Education Dean at Salter sprung an offer on me that it turns out I couldn't refuse. Salter had been waiting for me to complete my bachelor's degree, which I did the previous month at Worcester State University, after taking classes intermittently at three different colleges for nearly fifteen years. I had been teaching in the massage program for five years now, and evaluating other massage programs for almost three. Would I like to step up to the Interim Program Director position, Salter asked? The pay increase was negligible, but my hours would be bumped up significantly. My financial worries that had been plaguing me since I lost the Masterman's position were going to be a thing of the past!

Very shortly thereafter, my bank account began to grow. Bills were caught up. I was able to put a little money into a retirement account. Lots of plusses—but I quickly learned that some extra ca-ching does not necessarily equal happiness. Within months, Salter decided that they did not like my travel schedule. Too many Monday mornings missed while I was visiting my kids. I'd have to cut back on my ACICS visits, from fifteen per year to one or two, maximum. The schedule I had agreed to when I took the position was changed to the point that I would have to leave my loyal clientele at Worcester Fitness.

Those folks had been with me through the very lean times, almost never missing appointments, working around my crazy travel schedule. Threats from Salter started coming. "We're going to have to let you go if you don't commit to these hours. You now need to be here at this time, and this time, and this time." I almost caved. I got to the point of looking for a new massage therapist for my clients at Worcester Fitness because I didn't want to leave them hanging. It was comfortable to have a super steady income. I liked the students and the other teachers I worked with.

But, when it came down to it, that was all and it wasn't enough. I did some serious soul searching. I sought advice from my new crew of business peers and mentors, especially Tom. I didn't have the passion for teaching anymore, at least not at Salter. My business was growing. I had a job that allowed me to travel. In July of 2010, I made the decision to leave the director position. I knew it would hurt financially, but my dreams were coming true. I had to focus on Revitalize. I knew it was the only way to be true to myself. And for a year it did hurt. Every Monday, I would look at my schedule for the week, stressing out completely if my client goals weren't met.

As that first full year of Revitalize progressed, though, those weeks became fewer and farther between. I was forced to try new marketing ideas. Groupon and Local Deal reached out to me at a time when my coffers were getting low. A former student of mine appeared one day at the Post Office as I was buying stamps. I hadn't seen her in years, and asked if she was still doing massage. "A little," she said. But a series of unfortunate events, including an unexpected divorce leaving her as a single mother, had sapped her hope and drive.

I asked if she might be interested in filling in once in a while, or maybe help out doing couples massages. Although the road has been rocky for her, she has been on board ever since. Her client list continues to grow, along with her confidence. She is proud of her job, loves her clients, and has grown more as a person than I ever thought possible. All while helping Revitalize to expand our offerings.

So my massage business is doing well—growing to the point

that I am looking for a new, bigger location. I don't miss education administration. I see and live the power of putting positive vibes out into the world. Examples surround me. At the same time I discovered I needed a new roof on my house, my housemate's boyfriend moved in with her and started paying me extra rent. I received a free, random one-way ticket from JetBlue in my email inbox one day when I was feeling especially broke. Two ACICS trips occurred on opposite ends of a weekend I was planning to visit Minneapolis to do a twenty-four hour charity run—allowing me to fly there for free.

One time, a flight out of San Diego was delayed 10 hours on a beautiful day, while friends from Massachusetts just happened to be in town for a conference. We spent all day partying by the hotel pool. I made it to where I needed to go—just a little later.

I texted my friend, Colleen, last year to wish her a happy birthday. Turned out she was getting married in San Diego the next weekend, and didn't have any witnesses yet. I just happened to be going to San Diego to visit the kiddos—and they loved getting dressed up to go see a shotgun wedding. And, Colleen's husband—who happens to be a fantastic photographer—took an amazing family portrait that was better and more impromptu than anything I could have gotten done in a studio.

My brother, Joseph, was graduating from high school in 2008 and I was invited, but I didn't have the funds to make a special trip to Minnesota. Then I got an invitation to do a school evaluation in Minnesota the very same week.

Yes, the world is full of coincidences—or, the way I like to think of it is the stars aligning for me. When I injure myself—twist my knee, pull my back, tweak my neck—I see a positive. I may hurt, but it probably is temporary, and I have the chance to build empathy for my clients. I can say that I've been there, not just I've read or heard about that.

When I went through a divorce, I really didn't know how I would be able to go on. But now I can only see the bright side. I am happier. I have rediscovered the me that I'd lost. I have made so many friends that I never would have met. I have built a business that would have remained a dream.

I don't HAVE to travel to San Diego every month. I GET to travel to San Diego every month!! I helped write the book you are reading. I am still a young guy, and I really think the adversity I have been through pales in comparison to everyone else's in this book.

I've lost love. I've been broke. I've been depressed. But my story is everyone's story. Your problems are always the worst problems, and the most immediate because you are living them.

But don't give up. Keep moving forward and embrace your dreams. Smile when life squirts lemon in your eyes. Maybe it has just killed an infection that was forming!

Life is splendid and I am embracing it.

I hope you do, too!

∽

A Center of Influence
Nancy Dube

Nancy Dube owns and operates Dube Consulting, where she helps small businesses, offering technical expertise in the areas of strategic management, workforce planning and employment, employee relations, safety and risk management, and benefits and compensation. She has over 25 years of human resources experience in many fields. As a human resource manager, Nancy went out of her way to make employees feel valued.

Here, Nancy shares the story of how extricating herself and her children from an abusive marriage made her stronger and smarter.

I was married to an abusive ex-husband who led me to believe that I was inferior in everything I did. I was led to believe that I couldn't drive the car because I couldn't see at night, when it was dark. I did have trouble driving in the dark, but only because he had adjusted the headlights on the car to make sure that I couldn't see in the dark. I was led to believe that I wasn't a good mother. Yet, I was the one who got out of the abusive relationship to ensure the safety of my children. For many years, though, I was afraid to disobey him, so I gave in to his control.

How we met is a funny story. We met at a popular Worcester bar—The Boynton. My ex-husband was a cop, and he came into the bar one night after work for a drink. I was sitting at the bar with a friend, and so I started talking to the cop who sat down beside me. About a week later, he pulled me over with lights and siren going, and asked me out. So it all started with him being in control.

Soon into our marriage, he was controlling everything—including all the finances. When our daughter was born in 1987, he was out of work on disability. He started drinking heavily and had major mood swings. I had gone back to work after our daughter was born, but our neighbor saw his drinking and mood swings and told me about it. But, as happens so often in abusive situations, things got better for a while, and so I didn't do anything.

Four years later, though, after our son was born, things blew up again. He started abusing me and my daughter. I got restraining orders. LOTS of restraining orders. I needed police protection. But, he was on the police force, and the town cops—the "brotherhood of police"— tried to protect him. It was the State Police who really tried to help me. One day, my car broke down on Route 20. I had my arm outside the window, adjusting the CB antenna to get help. According to my three-year old, " a mean man in a red truck" hit us in the breakdown lane, severing my arm in several places. When I placed an emergency call for help, my husband heard the call over the police dispatch. He was working in that capacity on another police force. When the State Police arrived, I asked for a restraining order at the scene of the accident, before I was taken to the hospital, and again by phone to a judge while my arm was being sewn together. My abuser was in the lobby of the hospital.

I didn't tell anyone what was going on at first, because I was ashamed. I was a professional woman. I was working as a human resources manager. Honestly, though, when you are dealing with being beaten and being threatened, other people's problems seemed insignificant. Eventually, though, I did tell my parents, a counselor, and few close friends. Once I let the secret out, I didn't feel quite so alone, and I was able to start thinking more clearly.

The trigger that finally made me realize that I had to get out was the guns. While he was out on disability, my husband decided to become a gun dealer. This frightened me, because I knew he was violent and couldn't control his temper. It turned out that he was a "cop on the take." He came back to the house one night, cut the security alarm so that no one would know he was breaking in, and moved the guns from the house to the trunk of a police car. I was told that some of the town police actually helped him do this. That's when I knew I'd had enough. I wasn't the strongest person in the world at that point. But he made me strong. I had no choice—I had to save my life and my children's lives.

I spent the next five years in and out of court. And that's when I found out that the "brotherhood of judges" is stronger than the "brotherhood of police." I found judges who were willing to listen to me and believe me. Because I didn't trust him to be alone with the children, we arranged for court supervised visits. He did not elect the supervised visits, and chose to stop seeing his children from that point on. Child support payments stopped. He hasn't seen his kids in 18 years.

He caused immeasurable trauma and pain. The children and I needed an enormous amount of therapy. We got counseling at Daybreak and Jewish Family Services. My family and friends supported us. My faith got me through. One of my counselors told me to "honor your ex-husband, he is making you strong." I still hate him very much for being a bully. For not supporting my dreams. For being a controller and an aggressor.

And I hate him for what he did to the children. When the kids went outside to play, they wore whistles around their necks. One time, he drove by the house and pointed a gun out the car window at my daughter. Even today, she is hyper-vigilant. She is very aware of her surroundings. She watches everybody. She knows everything that's going on around her. My son was so very young when all this was going on that he experienced it only secondarily. He didn't experience the abuse first-hand, and he doesn't really remember it. It has only been in the past year that my son has asked to see pictures of his father. My daughter went to a special needs school, and my son has ADHD. Is this a result of their early home situation? Who knows? You don't necessarily see or realize the long-term problems when you are in the middle of it.

I was single for five years. We moved from Spencer to Worcester. We were poor. Before, I had been earning a six figure salary. Now I was working three jobs and earning $15,000 to support my family. I shopped for clothes at the Salvation Army. I spent a lot of time with the kids. They needed me. I was the only parent they had. My friends—many of whom were self-employed—really helped me. While I was at work, they would take the kids to their activities. And I would pick them up every night. You do what you have to do and make it work. I realized that if I could do this, then I could adapt to anything.

After five years, I met my current husband. I had enrolled the kids in Tae Kwon Do classes, because people told me that they needed a constructive way to deal with any aggression they might be feeling. He was an assistant instructor and taught the children. After working together for a year, we were married after six months. My husband was so completely different from my ex-husband. It takes a special man to be a father to someone else's children. He supported my dreams. One time, my husband said to me, "I don't know too many people as strong as you."

That's when I knew it would all be OK.

Four and a half years ago, I was laid off from my job. I was burned out and had had enough of Corporate America. I was frustrated by the long hours and the amount of work I was doing. I decided to go out on my own. I said to my husband, "I have the skills that can help other people in a down economy. I can help them with their resumes and job search. I can help business owners with the hiring, firing and HR needs" That's when Dube Consulting was born. I evolved during that first year in business. I didn't make enough money to live on, but I was learning about running a business and establishing my reputation. The second year was a little better. I made some money. Today, my business is thriving. I have a client base. I offer workshops and seminars for many different organizations and businesses. I am a regular contributor to *Worcester Business Journal.* I have built a network of support and resources, and help others with building human connections.

My husband has been very supportive. He encourages me, rather than discouraging me. Having a husband and children who support me in my dreams has helped me to stay focused on my target. Using the tools and gifts I have been given allows me to have flexibility and creativity in my life.

I have learned so much on this journey I have been on. First of all, if you are in a life-threatening situation, don't hide it. Come out and get support from people. Reach out to the resources that are available. It helps to talk it through. You don't have to share everything with your friends—but use them for support. I have helped many other women to get through their issues. My own experience has given me the compassion and the skills—I know. If one day at a time is too much, take it one hour at a time. Take it one step at a time—and if one step is too much, take baby steps.

Through support, counseling and prayer, I was able to find the support I needed. I embraced God and religion after not practicing for many years. I have held positions of leadership and dealt with other people's problems. I have overcome serious health issues for myself and my daughter. I mentor others, embrace relationships and friendships. I take risks—I built a business from the ground up by giving first of myself.

My creativity has grown a lot since I went into business. In some way, I make a contribution to every person I touch. Maybe it's listening. Maybe it's counseling. I am "a center of influence." That's one reason why I am so driven to get involved with women's organizations.

I have learned to take care of myself, and to take time for myself. I think nothing of getting a pedicure now! It's something I do for me.

It's important to have faith. When mine waivers, my husband's faith is there to sustain me.

Think positive. The glass is half full. When that one door closes, you will be stronger and smarter, and have more resources to overcome each new challenge.

Follow your passion, and you CAN do anything you want.

$\backsim$

CHAPTER 4

What Are Your Gratefuls Today?
Scott Erb and Donna Dufault

Scott Erb and Donna Dufault are the dynamic duo behind Erb Photography. Focusing on advertising, editorial, and commercial portraiture and product work, Erb Photo specializes in food, restaurant and hospitality clients. Together, Scott and Donna have over 40 years of experience working in photography. Scott has a degree from the SouthEast Center of Photographic Studies. In 2003, he founded the Worcester Photography Center, which counts over 500 members. He was the president of the Commercial Industrial Photographers of New England. Donna has a degree in fine art photography. She has worked at some of the best photographic printing labs in the country, and worked with some of the top art photographers in the world. Donna provides marketing and business development support for Erb Photography, as well as serving as studio manager and second shooter.

Here is their story:

Donna: Scott and I met in Rochester, New York, and worked together at a catalog sales company. For me, it was love at first sight! I worked in management, so I knew that the company was planning to close the Rochester office and move to California. I had already decided to move back to Massachusetts.

Scott: During the last month that Donna and I worked together, we put on a show of the works by the people who worked there. That's when we started spending a lot of time together. Two weeks before Donna left the company, we had the show. That's when I got to meet all her friends. My parents came. And it's a funny story. I got home that night, and my Dad came into my room and said, "I saw true love tonight. That girl, Donna, is so in love with you. She doesn't just like you. She's <u>really</u> in love with you. " I didn't have a clue!

Now, what is interesting in my life at that point was that I knew the company was closing. Coincidentally, my family was moving to Alabama for Dad's job. So I had a choice to make. Do I move to California with the company? Do I stay in Rochester? Do I move to Alabama with my family? Or, do I see how this very young relationship is going to happen?

Donna: The real story is that Scott had choices. We had only been dating for about a month when all this happened. I knew I was in love with him. But he wasn't aware of how I felt. Ultimately, Scott decided to follow me to Massachusetts. Things moved really fast. That seed of love grew like a flower. We moved to Peabody, but I was working for a fine art printing company in Worcester. Scott got a job at the same company, so we ended up moving to Worcester. And, before long, we were out of work. Both Scott and I were out of work at the same time. We had just gotten married— just getting our life going. It was scary.

Scott: This was at the time that digital photography was taking off. I had actually given up photography for a while because of the chemicals. I was getting sick all the time. We'd had some exposure to the digital world through that last job. But we weren't taking pictures that way. We were just printing them. So I decided to go back to school…to learn about this computer stuff. I started by taking basic courses at some of the local schools, and eventually got my certificate from Clark University's Computer Career Institute.

Donna: If Scott was going to go back to school, then I had to find a way to pay for it. This was during the time of the dotcom boom. That was the thing to do. The money was in the dotcom world. So I got a really excellent job with a dotcom in Waltham, because I had really good transferrable skills. And for the next 18 months, life was pretty good, although I very rarely saw Scott.

Then, in January, none of us saw this coming, because it was a very successful company—the company just closed. Our investors just decided they were done, and they wanted to get out before the bubble burst. That left 108 employees without jobs. I came home yet again and said to Scott, "I lost my job today. Again."

Eventually, I got another job here in Worcester, but I wasn't making as much money as at the dotcom. Scott was getting work assisting on photo shoots that really didn't pay much. But, he got to learn all about the digital photography world.

Not long after, my boss approached me and said, "Because of the down economy, we need a smaller operation." I said, "I can't really afford to take a pay cut. I guess I'll just have to look for a new job." Then I injured myself. It was the worst possible timing. I was let go. I really don't think that he let me go because of my injury, but it didn't help matters. So, there I was, back home again. That's when we started thinking, "What are we going to do? This keeps happening." It seemed like the entire time we were in Massachusetts, we had been looking for jobs.

Scott: In the meantime, 9/11 happened and all this other stuff. So the economy wasn't exactly blossoming. I was working for other photographers—one in particular. But he lost one of his biggest clients when their company moved to Florida. He lost a huge chunk of money, and he couldn't afford to keep me, either.

I had started building my own clientele by that point. And the truth is, after a certain point, when you say, "enough," you either decide that you're going to go out and do your own thing, or you're just going to be a photographer's assistant. And I was done. It's not that I didn't like the people. It was time to move on.

But I wasn't learning anything. I had already learned everything I needed to know, and basically doing their jobs for them. Which, in my opinion, is the best way to learn—when you are doing everything. It was great. I said, "Now I know how that guy works, and how that guy works, and that one, too. Now I can assimilate what I need for me."

Donna: But, that year, after being laid off for the fourth time, I was devastated. I thought it was the end of the world. I couldn't believe this was happening again—for the fourth time! I felt like a failure.

Scott: And you blamed yourself for it.

Donna: We were in financial meltdown. We were living on credit cards, and we got into some serious debt. We couldn't pay our mortgage. We had to ask our parents for help. I finally applied for unemployment benefits. At that time, though, the economy was so bad that you got only about a third of what you had been making. We didn't have enough money to make ends meet.

I was so depressed. I would send out 20 to 25 resumes every week, going through every possible job website. Some days, I couldn't even get out of bed. We would look at each other some nights and say, "We're going to end up out on the street." "We're going to have to move in with my parents." "We're not going to make it."

Scott's parents were living in Alabama. Then, my Dad died very unexpectedly. Naturally, we were completely unprepared and in shock. There were a lot of issues to deal with there.

Scott: We were dealing with so many issues all at once. The economy had crashed. We were under water with our mortgage.

We literally could not even sell our house. We owed money that we didn't have.

Donna: It was one thing after another. It just kept coming in waves. 2009 was probably the worst year of our lives.

Scott: Our parents and our friends—those who still had jobs—helped us through it. They would give us money to pay bills. They would bring us food, or take us out for dinner.

Donna: We were trying to keep just how desperate our situation was on the down low. But they all knew. We used to love going out, we were so outgoing. Now, we couldn't even go out for a drink with our friends. Our friends would come over and literally see no food in our cupboards. I would visit my Mom and say, "Can I take that box of pasta home?" It was pretty bleak.

Scott: But, we both knew from the start that we wanted to stick with photography—somehow. I had known since I was in the second grade that I wanted to be an artist of some sort. From that point on, I would draw, draw, draw, paint, and draw. I started dabbling in photography in high school. But never did I imagine that I would open my own photography business.

Donna: That is when we decided to invest in digital photography and it saved us. Scott didn't have to be in the darkroom all the time, with the chemicals. He could set up his computer anywhere and do the work. There were still some chemicals involved in the processing, but they were all inside a machine. He didn't even have to touch any of it.

Scott: That's what actually got me back into photography. But I had to learn everything all over again. I had no computer training. Almost all of the guys I was assisting were already into digital, or were just getting into it—so we all learned together.

Donna: I really pushed Scott to get back to his true passion. I'll take credit for that. When he told me about the chemical issues, I got that. But, now this whole new digital world opened up to us.

Scott: I have to say this—this wouldn't have happened if Donna hadn't supported me in my crazy ideas. She got behind me and said I could do all these things. She said all the right things—what I needed to hear.

Donna: I said, "If this is what you love to do, then let's go for it." Then I felt that I really had to look for a job so that Scott could do the things he really wanted to do.

Scott said, "Why don't you come and work for me?" I had all the right skills. But I just wasn't sure....

Scott: Donna wasn't in the right frame of mind at that moment. And, frankly, I wondered if I could afford this. I knew what our finances were. Could we both afford to work in the business? In the short term, I thought it would be OK. Well, once Donna made her commitment to the job, she made up her salary in the first year. She put herself in the position that you do what you can to make it work.

Donna: Once we got our work out there, we just kept going. We built a client base. In the spring of 2009, we were really busy. We said, "Oh my God, we did it!" But, then, because of the economy, many of our clients couldn't pay us. They were having their own problems. We understood that, but it didn't help us pay our credit card bills.

But, you know what? At the end of every day, we would say to each other, "What are you grateful for today?" That's how we would go to sleep every night, with the thoughts of what we are grateful for. And we are still here and thriving.

Scott: We definitely believe in the power of positive thinking. If you let yourself get into negative thoughts, it festers. And then you can't get yourself out of it. Negative is easy. Positive you have to work at!

So, good or bad, count your "gratefuls" at the end of every day. Tomorrow is a new day.

In the morning, we also give ourselves a pep talk—"this is going to be a great day today," "we're going to get some really good shots."

Donna: We try to put out there what we want to happen.

Whether it happens or not is irrelevant. But it puts you in the mindset to be able to deal with whatever you encounter.

We learned that it may be scary as hell to go out there on your own, but there is no one to lay you off, and your fate is in your own hands. And that is what is needed—taking control of your own life is truly a step each person should take. We learned that we are strong enough, and talented enough, and that we could make it. But, it takes a team. It takes support from your family and friends—and the good will of these folks. And we learned that networking is a key to our success.

Scott: We have a plan. And we know that as long as we have each other, we have everything we need. Once you realize that you don't need all this "stuff," you are free to accomplish everything you want. Right now, we are actively involved with the fledgling *Foodies of New England* magazine with Domenic Mercurio. It's up and running and we plan to take it national. Our ultimate goal is to be the co-owners of a national magazine.

Follow your bliss, your passion! If you are talented enough and follow your passion, you will go for it and achieve exactly what you want. It's about being happy, not about how much money you have or how many toys you have. If you have family, friends, and a job you love, you have everything!

Donna: Work hard and don't let yourself get blocked. But you also need to have fun. It is worth it. We may not be rich, but we are happy. We love our lives and we are grateful for every day.

When A Door Opens, I Like To Walk Through It
January Jones

January Jones is a speaker, author, radio personality and humorist. She has done radio and television interviews, promoting her theories on life with humor and hope. January hosts, "January Jones Sharing Success Stories" which is syndicated on TheIntertainmentNetwork.com and BlogTalkRadio.com. She is the author of "Thou Shalt Not Whine…The Eleventh Commandment," and three books on the Kennedy Assassination. She grew up in Detroit and attended the University of Detroit.

January tells her story:

In the mid-1960s, when I was a flight attendant for Eastern Airlines, I met and fell in love with David Beil—a Navy test pilot. We got married, and our daughter, Kelly, was born in 1966. We lived in California, and I was very content to be a stay-at-home wife and mother. Dave was sent to Vietnam for a year, and that experience led him to believe that he could survive anything. That was not to be the case....

When he left the Navy after his tour of duty in Vietnam, Dave became a test pilot for Lockheed, testing planes for use in Vietnam. In 1969, the unthinkable happened. Dave was tragically killed when a plane he was testing crashed. He was 32 years old. Kelly was 3; our second daughter, Brooke, was just 6 weeks old. And at age 25, I was a widow. Of course, Dave's death affected us all, but it affected Kelly's young life the most. She had a strong bond with her father, and all of a sudden, he disappeared. This was very difficult for a 3 year old to comprehend.

In many ways, though, we were fortunate. We were well-provided for financially, so I just had to support my family emotionally. We were also lucky to be a military family—I learned how to be a single parent during Dave's year in Vietnam. And I was lucky to have a very strong support network—being a military wife is like belonging to a sisterhood. Putting my life back together was a very, very slow process. But my best friend—also a military wife and like a sister to me—encouraged me to approach my healing process one day at a time, just putting one foot in front of the other.

When someone you love dies tragically and violently at a young age, it's like you have crashed into a brick wall and died yourself. People think you will get over it. But guess what? You never get over it. Forty-seven years later, I still wake up mornings thinking it's not true—Dave really wasn't decapitated in a helicopter crash. It's just a very, very bad dream. Forty-seven years later, it's always the last thing I think about before I fall asleep. You never get over it...never, ever, ever!

But you DO go on! One step at a time. One day at a time. And you do it for him. The worst thing for someone on the other side is if you can't cope, if you can't carry on. I don't know how I know this, but for me it is what it is. I'm not sure how it works this way, but it does. It's why I look forward to meeting Dave on the other side.

Within a year of Dave's death, I went to a Christmas party and met the man who would become my second husband, Leif Jonasson. Leif was an Army helicopter pilot, later becoming a commercial pilot for United Airlines. He was divorced and had a young son, Leif III. We were young and in love—and it must have been my destiny to fall in love with pilots! Did I have any apprehensions about falling in love with another pilot, after losing Dave? Of course I did—but I also realized that there is a big difference between being a test pilot and being an airline pilot. Leif and I got married in 1970, and had a child of our own—Mari—in 1972. We were the classic blended family—his, mine and ours. We had a wonderful life in California, including a beautiful house with a pool. I loved airline life.

But I always wanted to do something. My mother and grandmother had always worked. I came from a long line of working mothers. With two friends, I created a retail shop—Second String—which sold used sports equipment on consignment. Then Leif and I opened The Training Table, a restaurant in a sports complex. We also bought five "fixer upper" houses, renovated them, and then sold them. In 1982, I was a member of the Thousand Oaks Racquet Club, when the owner decided to retire. Leif and I bought it, and I was the manager there for 20 years. Just as I thought it was my destiny to meet and marry pilots, since I had always played sports while growing up in Detroit, I guess it was my destiny to work in sports-related businesses.

When a door opens, I like to walk through it. Leif and I were always eager to live an active life, so it was a very easy thing to do. The opportunities were there and we took them. When you are open to seeing opportunities and possibilities—when life flows—it works. By the time this book is published, I will be 70 years old—I have had a lifetime of doors opening. It's amazing how the universe works!

When I was in my early forties, I attended a charity event that featured a psychic. When he did my reading, he said, "What an interesting life you have ahead of you. You are going to be a writer." I had never considered that. I said to him, "What will I write about?" He replied, "When the time comes, you'll know what to write. You will write your first book when you are 50. But you won't be a success with it until you are in your late 60s."

◦

I had always been fascinated with the Kennedys, and followed everything they did. Then, when I became a widow myself, I was even more fascinated with Jackie as a widow. All of a sudden, it clicked! While I was researching the Kennedy family, I stumbled upon some information that indicated that Jackie had actually met Aristotle Onassis while she was still married to Jack. My first book, "Oh, No, Jackie O," was published when I was 50 years old! The book included a very controversial conspiracy theory—that Onassis had the resources available to orchestrate the Kennedy assassination. I was doing interviews all the time, and it was at this time that I took on the name and persona of "January Jones" to protect my family due to all the controversy. My second book was "Jackie, Ari and Jack: The Tragic Love Triangle." After my first two books about the Kennedys, I started in a different direction, and wrote "Thou Shalt Not Whine: The 11th Commandment," based on a survey of the Top Ten things that people whine about. It reached Number One at amazon.com. I became a whine-ologist!

While I was promoting my books, I stumbled into radio. I loved doing talk radio shows better than doing TV talk shows... because I could do the radio shows in my PJs! I was having so much fun! We sold the racquet club and decided to retire. I was going to play golf and eat chocolate. NOT!!! I became a radio talk show host, starting out with "Successimo," on BlogTalkRadio.com. Today, my show, "January Jones Sharing Success Stories," is syndicated on three networks, and I have over 1.6 million listeners! This is a career I had never planned on. I have no financial agenda. I am doing this because I love it. I love sharing inspiration with others.

I have learned so much about myself and about life through all of my experiences. I never thought I would have a Number One book on amazon.com. I never thought that I would be a successful radio host. But I was brave enough to walk through those doors when they opened to me. My personal mantra is, "If you can think it, you can do it!" It is never easy. You have to have the ability to realize when you are going down the wrong path. It takes energy. It takes networking. It takes a lot of inspiration. But follow your passion. "What do I really want to do? I'd like to do radio." Put that out to the Universe, and it will happen. Radio is my passion. And my passion for radio and inspiration flow into my books. My next book will include interviews I have done with some of my most inspiring radio guests who are Priceless Personalities—including Tom Ingrassia!

Walk through every door that opens to you. Be a traveler. And live life with love and lots of laughter.

❧

Trust The Journey
Shandirai Mawokomatanda

Shandirai Mawokomatanda—Shandi—is pastor at Wesley United Methodist Church, in Worcester, Massachusetts, where he leads a multicultural, urban congregation. He was born in Zimbabwe, and he immigrated to the United States in 1992.

Shandi shares his story here for the first time.

Let me preface this by saying that I have not shared this particular part of my story with too many people—not even with some members of my family. I have shared some aspects of my story on two occasions during sermons at two of the churches I have served. At those times, I felt empowered to share in that particular setting and format because I knew that there were others who were struggling with similar issues that I had struggled with. Even then, however, I questioned to myself whether sharing such deeply personal experiences in that format was the right way. I am a private person, and because so much of my life as a pastor is on display for all to see, I try to protect my private life as much as possible. I am sharing my story here in order to provide hope, healing and inspiration to others who may face similar circumstances—to say, you are not alone.

I was born in Zimbabwe in 1978. My family was large—well, small by Zimbabwean standards!—I was the sixth of seven children. My father was a pastor, now retired. So I grew up in the church. My parents home—the parsonage—was always open to anyone who needed a place to stay. We often had guests.

It took me a long time to understand what transpired in my life to wreak so much havoc and trauma.

When I was 9 years old, there was an incident where one of the guests who was living with us took me aside into the bathroom one evening, and proceeded to molest me. I was not certain what was happening at the time. And I did not tell anyone. But that incident left an imprint on me. As the days and years progressed, I struggled to understand what had happened—and why. I am still trying to understand.

Soon, I began acting out, protesting against what had happened to me—at least that's what my counselor told me. I started stealing from my parents. At first, I stole small things, but then I started stealing bigger things. My parents took me for counseling. It was not until years later that the counselor said to me that the stealing was a call for attention, but that I didn't know how to ask for that attention. Still, I didn't reveal the reason for my acting out.

When I would steal, I knew it was wrong and so I would be plagued by guilt. I felt so much guilt and shame that I would often go into the church sanctuary and cry my heart out to God. "God, please make me stop!" This sense of guilt and shame affected my already-fragile self-esteem. I felt unworthy of God's love, unredeemable. I prayed and hoped for change, but I would find myself stealing again. I began to feel that my life was a lost cause.

When I was 10, my parents moved to the United States for one year, on a mission trip, leaving me and my younger sister behind to live with our older sister. I continued to act out under the care of my sister—still not understanding why. When my parents returned to Zimbabwe, we moved to a different town. Prior to our move, I had been very social, and had done well in school. When we moved, however, I had another traumatic experience that transformed my personality. It was on the first day of school. I was the new kid. To compensate for my discomfort at being in a new environment, I became overconfident—and pointed out to the teacher a mistake he had made in a lesson on the blackboard. The teacher thanked me for catching the mistake, and as he turned back to the board to correct it, I turned to the rest of the class and took a bow—which the teacher saw! "I don't know what you did in your old school, but we don't do that in this school," the teacher said. Then he proceeded to slap me. The other kids teased me afterward, and I retreated into myself and shut down. Consequently, it became more difficult for me to express myself.

Three and a half years later, my family moved to the United States permanently, settling in northeastern Pennsylvania. I was now in an entirely new culture and environment. My sister and I were the only two black kids in school. While I adjusted comfortably in the new school, a year later my parents sent me to boarding school. This was yet another change in my young life, and I didn't deal with it well. I retreated even further into myself and found it difficult to make friends. I would often lock myself in my room and hide myself away from the world. I did have a roommate. My roommate was a young man from Lithuania—a rather brilliant student who was rather poor by the standards of this boarding school. For instance, he had only two outfits of clothing, which he would alternate to wear every other day. The other students often teased him because of this. I was about his only friend.

At this point in my life, it wasn't just that one incident of having been molested that was traumatic. Even these smaller traumas seemed like major traumas, because I had not quite learned how to cope well. I had continual intervals of wrestling not only with my shame and guilt, but also with my identity in the world.

I decided to play sports as a way to become more social. I made some friends and even managed to find a girlfriend. While my social life improved significantly by the time I was in my senior year of high school, I continued to wrestle with my internal demons. I began to confront them when, one day, I found out my girlfriend had also been molested as a child. She confided in me about her experience, shared about her struggle with depression, and how she was seeing a school counselor. Hearing about my girlfriend's experience opened up a lot of what I had been repressing.

I was 15 years old when I attempted suicide for the first time. One Saturday evening, I went to the local convenience store and bought as many bottles of pills as I could. I returned to my room and took them. It was a weekend when very few people were around. I was by myself and had no roommate at the time. After taking the pills, I decided to fall asleep, hoping never to wake up. Fortunately, I became rather sick and vomited so much that I imagine I got rid of any toxins from the pills. I welcomed the pain of feeling sick as though I was torturing myself. Eventually, I recovered from the sickness, and I never told anyone what I had done. The aftermath produced the same feelings I experienced in my younger days. This suicide attempt began to haunt me, feeding my longstanding feelings of shame and guilt, and of being unworthy and unlovable. I felt like a horrible person.

At the end of our senior year, many transitions were in play, including a break up with my girlfriend. It was very difficult breaking up, because I had grown rather attached to her for deeper reasons than love alone. She had been the first person I felt understood how I felt, even though I had never mentioned a word to her about my experience. The break up was unavoidable, and it was inevitably difficult on me. We were graduating from high school and going off to college. We also had significant differences that made our relationship impossible to sustain. She was Muslim. I was Christian. This became yet another trauma for me to try to deal with. I had separation anxiety. I could not bear the thought of being parted from her. So, I considered converting to Islam, but I had such deep roots in Christianity that I could not forsake something that formed such a big part of my identity. I tried majoring in a discipline with lucrative career opportunities—computer science, engineering—so that her family might accept me even though I was not Muslim. Everything fell apart, however, when I began failing my courses—because I was not happy with the career direction I was taking. I stayed in touch with my girl-friend, and we even talked about marriage after college. Eventually, her family found out about our relationship and they were not happy. Her mother gave her an ultimatum—it was either me or her—and if she chose me, she would be disowned. We had no choice but to end the relationship. This rejection made me feel as though something was hideously wrong with me. I felt contemptible. I felt unwanted.

While dealing with the anxiety of having been separated from the one person I felt understood my experience, I felt I had been abandoned to deal with my inner demons alone. When I went to college, my freshman year felt very much similar to my first year at boarding school. This time, rather than isolate myself, I joined the college choir and a fraternity. But, it was disheartening to know that, although many people surrounded me, I still felt so alone and isolated.

During my sophomore year, I was a Resident Assistant in the dorm. That meant I had my own room, and so once again, I found it easy to isolate myself. While I had joined the fraternity, I seldom spent time with them. I tried a new relationship, but she transferred to a different college. By the end of my sophomore year, I was feeling lost and alone. I even lost touch with my faith, partly because of the doubt provoked in me when I began to explore Islam. I had always taken my Christian faith for granted, but now I felt I had lost that, too. Alone and isolated, I felt that God was far from me; that God was not hearing me. I did not know what to do or where to turn.

That's when I attempted suicide for the second time.

The saving grace is, I have an aversion to pain—physical pain—so I did not want to try anything violent this time. All I wanted to do was to fall asleep. In my depression, I slept a lot. It was when I was most at peace when I was asleep. I had no worries, no fears. So I prayed to fall asleep and never wake up. Again, I went to the local drug store and I purchased over the counter sleeping pills and took as many as I could. Again, they did not do anything except make me sick. I fell asleep and when I woke up, I vomited. Déjà vu.

The following year—fall semester of my junior year—I tried to fall asleep again for the third time. This time, I took the pills and decided that I would go for a drive on some of the back roads of Pennsylvania. I was looking for a cliff to drive over, and I hoped I would just drift off, fall asleep at the wheel, and that would be the end of it. As I drove in the middle of the night, I discovered, though, that I was driving toward New York, where my parents were living. I stopped the car and turned around to go back to my dorm room. Upon my arrival, I fell sick and, once again, I vomited.

This time, however, other students realized that something was wrong. I was not responsive. They didn't know what I had done, though. I always took care to throw away all the pill bottles, so that it would look like I had just died in my sleep. That's what I wanted my family to think. A friend found me and called 911. I was taken to the hospital by ambulance. They ran a series of tests, including giving me a spinal tap. Surprisingly, they could not find anything in my system—probably because I had thrown every-thing up earlier. My parents were called and came to the hospital.

When I finally woke up and saw my family and friends in my hospital room, I realized for the first time that I had people in my life who loved me. I was not really alone. I saw the love and support of people who I thought had never noticed me before. I was humbled by the love and care of my friend, who cleaned my room after the mess, and prepared for my homecoming. I felt that I was waking up for the first time to see how much God had blessed me with.

That experience turned my life around. I changed majors—to a self-designed, interdisciplinary major in social services—and began feeling some pride in my work. My academic advisor—who also was Dean of Students—pointed me in the direction of volunteer work with the Salvation Army and United Way. When I graduated, she was instrumental in advocating for me to get my first job offer—with the United Way. I was humbled. The job with the United Way was a saving grace. I felt that I was making a difference in the world. I was on community task forces and boards. I got to see first hand the struggles people face every day. It helped my sense of self worth.

While working with the United Way, I attended a conference on children and poverty. The keynote speaker was a Catholic priest. In his keynote address, he said something that would catapult me into a new direction. Speaking to human service professionals who sometimes have to tow the line between church and state, he said to us, "If you want to make a real and lasting difference in the lives of the people you serve, you have to put God back in the center of their lives. That is the only way things will ultimately change."

This was my Aha! Moment. I approached the speaker after his session, and found myself hanging around him. When he noticed me, he invited me to sit with him for lunch. As we talked, I said something that surprised me. "I feel that God is calling me to do something more," I said. I do not know where those words came from. I had always resisted God's call.

That same day, I received a call from my parents, saying that my grandmother's health was failing, and they didn't think she would make it much longer. My father could not leave his congregation, so I needed to return to Zimbabwe—for the first time in about eight years—to attend to my grandmother's needs and funeral arrangements. That trip opened my eyes to see the suffering of the people of my country. This was a life transforming experience—an affirmation that God was calling me, and that he had prepared a path for me.

When I returned from Zimbabwe, I made the decision to attend seminary, with the intention of going into mission work. I also started the ordination process, although I did not want to become a pastor. That first year at seminary was tough—it was awful, in fact. I went into another major depression. Again, I isolated myself, coming out of my room only to eat (when I did eat), and to go to class. It was in seminary that I decided—for the first time—to seek counseling to help me with the many issues I was dealing with.

While in seminary, I received other affirmations. I had teachers affirm in me gifts for teaching. They inspired me to consider pursuing advanced studies. There was just one problem— I had no funding to pay my tuition. My family supported me during my first year at Boston University, but that put a financial strain on them. By the start of my second year in seminary, my family had run out of money and could no longer support my tuition. I was in the States on a student visa, so I could not legally work off campus to make money. I was considering working illegally when I received a call from a United Methodist New England Conference District Superintendent, offering me a job as a student pastor for a church in northern Maine. Even though this would require a four hour commute to Boston for classes, it was the answer to my financial dilemma and immigration predicament.

From that experience, I fell in love with pastoral ministry. The rest, as they say, is history.

Looking back, I realize now that it was my personal relationships that kept me going through three suicide attempts and the other issues I was dealing with. My relationship with my high school girlfriend kept me going after my first attempt. Knowing about her experience gave me a reason to know that I was not alone, and that someone else could understand my struggles. The overwhelming love and support of my friends and family also helped me find new strength after my attempts in college. I know it was the case after my third—and most serious—attempt.

New relationships after college also sustained me. While I was working at the United Way, I met an amazing woman named Sandy. I was Sandy's supervisor—even though she was forty years my senior. And she was like a mother to me. In fact, all the women in the office tried to mother me! When I told Sandy that I was leaving my job to start seminary, she teared up as she began telling me that God had a plan for my life, and that I would do amazing things. Sandy became the most significant saving grace in my life.

While at seminary, I called Sandy every night, and would tell her about my struggles. She was the first person I told about being molested as a child back in Zimbabwe. I had not even told my family, because I did not want my parents to feel guilty for opening our home to someone who would abuse me. It was Sandy who urged me to seek pastoral counseling to deal with this issue that continued to haunt me. I was able to see a pastoral counselor, who helped me to accept that I cannot change the past, to acknowledge what had happened, and to find courage to let it not haunt me. I am so grateful for Sandy and for the countless people who helped me along the way.

There is an African proverb that says, "A person is a person through and with other persons." I am who I am because of the relationships I have had. They have formed me and, sometimes, transformed me.

If I am to summarize what I have learned through all of these experiences—and what I want to share with others—it comes down to look around…see…and listen. Keep your eyes open. There was so much beauty and love around me that I did not recognize for far too long. I also have a lot of love to give. I learned that other people often see things in us that we do not see in ourselves. Certainly my family, friends, Sandy, and others saw potential in me that I did not acknowledge. We are invited to listen to the wisdom of others. I remember now that a high school teacher once told me that I would go into the ministry. At the time, that was the farthest thing from my mind! But look where I am now.

Our lives are a journey, and on that journey there are inclines and declines, twists and turns. The important thing is to keep moving forward, even when it feels like the journey is leading you through a detour. Even those detours have something to teach us about ourselves and about other people. There is a saying that I like very much because it describes my journey. The saying goes, "Some people come into your life for a reason. Some people come into your life for a season. And some people come into your life for a lifetime." You never know for which purpose someone enters your life until you have shared the journey with them. The purpose may be revealed along the journey or at the journey's end. Whatever the case, know this: you are never alone on your journey. God always puts people on your pathway to accompany and guide you. In fact, that is God's own promise, to accompany us in our journeys. "When you pass through the waters, I am with you; and through the rivers, they shall not overwhelm you; when you walk through fire you shall not be burned, and the flames shall not consume." (Isaiah 43:2) "Lo, I am with you always." (Matthew 28:20)

Trust your journey.

Mind Over Body
Ken McDonnell

Ken McDonnell is a husband, father, triathlete—and public relations director for Wake Up Narcolepsy, a nonprofit supporting narcolepsy awareness and research. In October, 2007—just two weeks after completing a triathlon—Ken was riding his mountain bike in Oakham, MA, when a car struck him from behind. Ken has no recollection of the accident or the next five weeks. He was air-lifted to UMass Medical Center, in Worcester, MA, where a team of trauma specialists saved his life, and where his saga began, through life support, risky surgery, lengthy rehab and finally back from the abyss.

Here's how Ken tells the story:

I was 15 when I started running on my high school track team, and I've been a competitive athlete ever since. I've run half a dozen marathons, with a personal best time of 2 hours, 47 minutes. But in 1985 I gave in to the punishment of the marathon and started competing in triathlons, often with my twin brother, Steve, and sometimes with my wife, Deborah, after their marathon days were also behind them.

On October 14, 2007—just two weeks after I had completed a triathlon—I headed out for a leisurely mountain bike ride in Rutland State Park, not far from my home in Holden, in central Massachusetts. It was a beautiful fall afternoon, and I spent most of the ride on the miles of trails and service roads within the park. At one point, though, I had to venture onto Route 122, a two-lane highway that runs outside the park, to get to another section of the trail. My plan was to ride just a couple of miles on 122 and then head back into the park.

What happened next I don't remember. According to an eyewitness, a woman driving at about 50 miles per hour wandered into the breakdown lane, where I was riding, slamming into me from behind. The witness said I was thrown onto the car's windshield, then high into the air before crashing to the pavement. It's a miracle that I wasn't run over as well. My bike was thrown across the guardrail into the woods and was destroyed. My bike helmet broke in half. In and out of consciousness, I repeatedly tried to stand but kept collapsing. I often wonder whether I sensed the impact as it was happening.

According to the police report, the driver seemed in shock herself and couldn't or wouldn't acknowledge her involvement in the incident. She had zero financial assets, so in the end we were able to collect only about $20,000, the minimum insurance coverage she needed to license her car. And she was sentenced to just a year of probation and community service. So much for the status of cyclists.

My bleak condition dictated that I reach a trauma center quickly, so I was flown the 25 miles to the University of Massachusetts Medical Center's Trauma Unit, in Worcester. It's likely that "my" helicopter flew over our house in Holden on its way to

UMass. So Deborah, who was at home at that moment, may have heard the engine, though emergency responders would not contact her for several hours. To this day, when a life-flight 'copter flies over the house (they're all uniquely wide-bodied), I think to myself, "Been there, done that."

I'd been gravely injured – severe pelvic fractures, multiple cracked vertebrae and broken ribs, massive internal bleeding, a renal artery aneurysm, a collapsed lung, and a fractured skull and traumatic brain injury (TBI). Deborah later told me the doctors took her and our son, Cody, aside in those dark first hours to tell them my chances of surviving that first night were just 25%. They explained that brain injuries like mine release huge amounts of adrenaline and other stress hormones. This puts tremendous stress on the heart. In fact, I learned later that most people who die from traumatic brain injuries like mine expire from a heart failure.

For several weeks I required the help of a ventilator to breathe. On top of everything else, I developed a devastating lung infection. If my other injuries couldn't kill me, the infection nearly did. For the next five weeks, I was kept in a medically induced coma to manage pain and keep me still until I stabilized sufficiently for the necessary surgery on my pelvis. Since I had not yet regained consciousness, I wasn't yet aware of the severity of my injuries, and to this day I have no recollection of those five weeks.

The first thing I do remember was waking up at Fairlawn Rehabilitation Center, in Worcester, to which I had been discharged from BMC. I spent the next three months in a wheelchair, eventually graduating to crutches, and then a cane.

But as I lay in the coma, rehab was far off and certainly not a certain thing. Deborah diligently kept our family and friends around the country updated on my condition. As my doctors later told me, she was the most intense patient advocate they had ever seen. No surprise there. Our other son, Tyler, flew in from Florida that first night, as did Steve, my sister, Suzanne, and brother John.

Coincidentally, and pivotally, Dr. Sandra Proctor, a close friend and orthopedic surgeon, was scheduled to arrive in Boston from California the next day to attend a medical conference. When she landed, she came immediately to the hospital. After looking at my x-rays and realizing the severity of my pelvic injuries, it was immediately clear that I would need extensive and risky surgery to reconstruct the pelvis. She consulted with a colleague, Dr. Paul Tornetta, a trauma surgeon at Boston Medical Center (BMC). Dr. Tornetta was, again coincidentally, scheduled to make a presentation at the same conference. He concurred with Sandy's assessment and agreed to perform the surgery if I could be transferred to BMC. As the days passed, Deborah faced the agonizing decision whether to have UMass handle the procedure or move me to BMC for the surgery, a procedure that would determine whether I might ever walk again, let alone get back on a bike.

I was still on life support, making a transfer of this nature was exceedingly risky. Ultimately, though, once my condition had stabilized, Deborah's instincts and her respect for Sandy's guidance and Dr. Tornetta's reputation clarified the choice. I was transported into Boston by ambulance, with an ICU nurse by my side, manually "bagging" the portable ventilator to keep me breathing.

Ah, yes, my pelvis. The sacrum, the large, triangular bone connecting the pelvis with the spine, was fractured, and the right-side sacroiliac (SI) joint – connecting the sacrum with the ilium, the large, pan-shaped part of the pelvis – was dislocated. In addition, the pubis symphysis, joining the two front rings of the pelvis bone, normally joined by a half-inch of cartilage, had also been torn apart by the impact, resulting in a two-inch separation.

The UMass trauma team had given me an external fixator, a frame-like device screwed to either hipbone through the skin, to begin the crucial realignment of my crumpled pelvis. At BMC, before the surgery could begin, Dr. Tornetta removed the fixator and put my right leg in traction to aid the alignment. But he discovered that one of the fixator points had become infected, requiring a pump to handle the discharge from the wound. More delay. The infection addressed, finally I was ready for surgery. Remember, I still haven't regained consciousness.

To repair the pubis symphysis, Dr. Tornetta made a horizontal eight-inch incision a few inches below my navel, retracted my bladder, and then set the bones. To keep things in place, he inserted a titanium plate held by six screws into the bones.

Then, during the same surgery, he essentially screwed the SI joint back together with two eight-inch screws to re-attach the pelvis to the sacrum. This procedure was particularly risky due to the critical bundles of nerves in that area, whose proper function is necessary for walking, penile erection and continence. Fortunately, today all is well down there. And because the surgery came three weeks following the accident, the procedure was particularly difficult and time consuming – six hours in all.

As I said, I have no recollection of anything that happened during that time. Finally and gradually I emerged from the five-week drug cocktail confused, disoriented, frightened. For the two weeks I was at Fairlawn Rehab, I was well treated, though little physical therapy could take place because I was not yet permitted to place any weight on my right, damaged side. I was discharged on November 21, the day before Thanksgiving, giving that Thursday special meaning. I spent the next three months at home in a wheelchair, eventually graduating to crutches, then a cane and finally unaided back on two feet.

I diligently followed doctors' orders to stay off my right side. I'm confident my good behavior – and extraordinary medical care from day one – played a key role in enabling me to stand and walk the day my schedule said I could try. Dr. Tornetta later told me some patients require months of painful rehab before they can even stand unaided. I was back in the pool swimming laps (cautiously, mind you) two weeks later.

At the time of the accident, I had been working to get a solo PR business off the ground, so my financial situation would have been sketchy if it were not for Deborah's solid career as a financial planner.

Six years after my accident, thanks to my team of medical miracle workers, I can honestly say I have no long-term or noticeable physical disabilities. I've been able to regain almost 100% of my pre-accident strength and endurance, and I've competed in six triathlons, including the grueling Escape from Alcatraz race. The Escape is a 1.5-mile swim in the 52-degee waters of San Francisco Bay from Alcatraz Island, a hilly 18-mile bike ride, and an all-out eight-mile run.

I hope it doesn't come across as boastful, but I definitely believe the physical and emotional strength that I developed through all those years of consistent, diligent training carried me from the deathbed to the Escape finish line. I'd "escaped Alcatraz," and I'd also escaped death.

In a real sense, the payoff of all those miles and hours of training was a heart strong enough to survive the effects of the TBI. I could easily have ended up severely disabled or dead. Naively, I know, it never occurred to me that I might not recover fully. I was able to return to some triathlon training within six months after the accident, and I completed my first post-injury race within a year.

Though I've recovered well physically, the traumatic brain injury has been a tougher slog. The impact had caused bleeding in my brain in multiple locations. I hit the pavement on the left front of my forehead, the area of the prefrontal cortex, where executive functions reside, like organization, judgment and impulse control. For several years after, I was dissatisfied with my equilibrium, such as when I turned my head suddenly, but physical therapy has helped. Impulse control was troublesome for a year; I cried often and intensely, and I was unusually short-fused. Thankfully much of this has abated.

This "adventure" has shown me just how phenomenal the human brain is. We've evolved in such a way that brain can find new channels for many of the functions that may otherwise have been damaged beyond repair. This wonderful plasticity, however, regrows brain function, to the extent it can, much more slowly than bones and muscles heal.

I continue to struggle with short-term memory issues, typical for my type of TBI. And while my long-term memory is pretty much in tact, I often find myself not trusting this memory, making daily life frustrating. Through intensive cognitive therapy at Spaulding Rehabilitation Hospital, in Boston, I learned how to anticipate my anger and anxiety, and stay organized. The "blues," another symptom of TBI, come and go, but I've become familiar with their onset and can usually deal with the downs.

Difficult as it is to acknowledge, I am subtlety different now, though it's hard for me to recognize these changes. All we know is what we know at this moment, so I can't know exactly what I was like "BA," (before accident). This makes me more self-conscious. I worry that people may see me differently than I think I am. Do I appear strange or odd? This kind of thing threatens your sense of psychic balance and self-esteem.

Professionally, long-time colleagues tell me, when I ask them, that they don't see any fall-off of performance. Of course I hope they're not just being kind. But then, what if they did see a problem? Socially, I am less comfortable than I used to be. I feel less confident thinking on my feet, and I sometimes struggle to find words. I can feel these things happening, and I try to compensate, but I'm sometimes a little exasperated. Do these people think I have a problem? Am I sharp as I used to be? Usually yes, sometimes perhaps not so much.

10-14-07 has, however, brought some very good things to pass. BA, I had worked in public relations at Digital Equipment Corporation, and then EMC Corp, as well as Worcester Polytechnic Institute. Once I recovered from my injuries, I decided to start my own company—Mobius Connect Business Communications.

About a year ago, I met Monica Leahy Gow, who brought

me on as the full-time communications director with the non-profit organization she founded and runs, Wake Up Narcolepsy. I'm responsible for public outreach to promote Wake Up's mission to raise narcolepsy awareness and fund medical research. I handle website and social media content, graphic design, press relations, and lots more—all the skills I developed over 30 years in the corporate arena—for an organization dedicated to helping people with a debilitating, lifelong sleep condition. Lifelong…debilitating —situations I've come to know something about.

My experience dealing with my own cognitive issues has helped me to make a connection with people who have narcolepsy, a poorly understood and seriously mis-diagnosed neurological disorder. In fact, Monica has told me that my demonstrated ability to overcome adversity was the deciding factor in hiring me. I like to joke that I went through hell to land this job!

Somehow, I've never looked at my recovery from the accident as a "battle," though clearly I look on this from the perspective of successfully getting back to "normal." I came close to death. I'm fortunate to be walking—much less going for a swim, bike ride or run.

I've learned in no uncertain terms that no one is immune to crisis, and it can always be worse. Recent events—especially the 2013 Boston Marathon bombings—have shown me how lucky I am. Wake Up Narcolepsy had a team of charity runners in the Marathon—including Jared Chrudimsky, whose story you'll also read in these pages. I was in Boston that day to watch our runners cross the finish line, so I was very near the horror. That awful day will forever remind many of us of 9/11 and JFK. I remember exactly what I was doing. My own misfortune has made me much more sensitive to the suffering of others.

I have been incredibly fortunate to have a caring, supportive network of family, friends, colleagues and physicians. Throughout my recovery, the outpouring of concern from so many people— ranging from my extended family, to kids from grade school—has been overwhelming. Do I harbor fury toward the woman whose negligence put me here? You bet I do. But I don't allow myself to go to that dark place very often.

To this day—six years later—when people ask me how I'm doing, I always respond, "ancient history."

Expect the worst, hope for the best. It's an attitude I've assumed from almost 50 years of endless athletic training and competition, and from my upbringing. Wisdom comes from the journey, rather than from merely reaching the destination. Slowly gaining the confidence that I can sustain a pace through the pain and doubts. Mind over body. This isn't something I consciously think about. It's who I am. It's who all of us can be.

∽

CHAPTER 8

Celebrate Your Life
June Monteiro

June Monteiro is a member of The Toys, the legendary 1960s Girl Group, which also included lead singer, Barbara Harris, and Barbara Parritt. In 1965, The Toys topped the charts for six weeks with "A Lover's Concerto," whose instrumental track is based on a classical piece by Bach. The group followed up "A Lover's Concerto" with a second hit, "Attack." Through the ups and downs of her life, June has always remained in the entertainment industry. Currently, Barbara, June and Barbara are in the process of reforming The Toys.

June shares a story many have not heard before:

Being a part of a legendary '60s Girl Group was a dream come true for me! For as long as I can remember, I always wanted to be an entertainer. My Mom played the organ and piano. My Dad played violin and guitar in a band. The violin was his favorite instrument. When I was six years old, Dad started taking me with him to club dates, where I sang and danced while his band played. And people threw quarters at me. Even at that young age, I realized the joy that singing brought to people.

I grew up in Queens, New York, and attended Van Buren High School. When I was eleven years old, my Dad died. I was very upset by this, and went to live with my older sister, Gloria. I stayed with Gloria until I was fifteen. Gloria lived right next door to Barbara Parritt. Barbara and Barbara Harris went to Woodrow Wilson High. Barbara Parritt, her sister Alise, and I used to sing together every day. We also met Donald Gatling, and he used to sing with us, too.

At first, Barbara Parritt and I formed our group with two other singers. But one of them missed too many rehearsals, and we brought in Barbara Harris to replace her. Our manager, Bob Yorey named us The Charlettes, and we started performing at high school dances, record hops, and local talent shows. Bob got us our first record in 1960, when we were thirteen, fourteen, and fifteen years old. It was "The Fight's Not Over," backed with "Whatever Happened To Our Love?" Barbara Parritt sang lead on both songs. Eventually, we got work as background singers. Bob Crewe, who worked with The Four Seasons, heard us and decided to feature us on our own. We were re-christened The Toys, and went into the recording studio in 1965. All three of us sang lead, although it is Barbara Harris' voice on all of our hits. We were signed to the Dyno Voice label, and our first single was "A Lover's Concerto," which climbed the charts in the fall of 1965. Not only was the song Number One for six weeks, it also was the inspiration for The Supremes' sixth Number One record, "I Hear A Symphony"! We were on top of the world. We toured England and Europe. It was wonderful!

The Toys were performing at a supper club in Cleveland, opening for Lou Rawls. Melvin Franklin, of The Temptations, told me that I had to go and see Sly and The Family Stone. He said they were like nothing you've ever heard in music yet. "I know your group likes different beats and concepts," he said. "They have that same kind of concept. But over the top. I know you will love them."

The other girls didn't want to go—they went to see The O'Jays. So, I went—and it was a show you couldn't even put into words. I went backstage after the show and met Sly, and we clicked like we'd known each other all our lives. From that night, we grew very close to each other. We talked on the phone. He would tell me where his group was playing, and I would go and meet him there.

Eventually, we signed with Stone Flower Productions, and Sylvester "Sly" Stone was going to write us a hit song. I went out to California to meet with Sly, planning to stay for just two weeks. I went to the recording studio with Sly every day, and kept asking him, "when are you going to write that hit song for us?" Sly kept saying, "Oh, yeah, I'll get to it." Two weeks went by. Then a month. At the end of the second month, he finally came up with a song, "Love Is A Movie Star." And once he started working on it, I wasn't going anywhere until he finished it! But he kept changing it. Then he said, "I really can't get into this right now. My mind's not into it." In the meantime, I had now been away from my group for a couple of months, and Barbara and Barbara brought in another singer to temporarily replace me for live performances until I got back to New York.

I was with Sly in the studio every day when he was recording his first album for Clive Davis—trying to get him to finish our song. I was one of the "guys." I wasn't one of his women. I talked with him about music. I was there when he wrote all those great songs after his first hit, "Dance To The Music." I was with him at the Gorham Hotel, in New York City, when he wrote "Hot Fun In The Summertime." But I could see that he was being reckless.

Before I knew it, Sly and his crew were snorting cocaine. I didn't do it right away, but I saw that it helped to keep them up all night in the studio. I had now been in California for about six months, and Sly just wore me down trying to keep up with him. Eventually, he started passing me the box of cocaine. And soon, I was snorting out of my own box. At first, I said to myself, "let me see what this is all about.' Then, I didn't even know what planet I was on. Before long, I didn't know what day, week or month it was. Three years went by like three weeks.

I never did get back to the girls. I didn't want to go back home without the song. So Barbara Harris got her cousin to replace me, and the group continued to sing while I was out there with Sly. Before I knew it, time had passed and I did go back to New York. But then I went right back out to California. Sly said he was ready to do it. "We'll send for the other girls," he said. I was there for another year. The other girls kept asking me, "When is he going to send for us?" And every week, Sly would answer, "next week.' Then, "at the end of the month." And on it went.

My life wasn't so beautiful any more. The next thing I knew, I was really messed up on coke. It became my life. I didn't even know what I was out there for. I was just hanging out with Sly. He had his own house and recording studio in Bel Air, so I moved there and lived in one of the three cottages on the property.

Now that I was living alone, I was able to stop using coke. I got my head together. I went to some acting workshops in Los Angeles. That's where I met Patricia Pope. Pat had written a play, "Where Black Folks Live." At about the same time, there were some shootings on Sly's property. One night, I started hearing gun shots over the fence. Someone was shooting his dogs and the peacocks. I hid in the wine cellar. That's when I knew I had to get out. Otherwise, I might end up dead. I went to stay with Pat, and she nursed me back to health and helped me pull myself together. I didn't want my family to see me like that. You can imagine my state of mind when I finally left Sly after three years. I never wanted to go back to that life again!

The girls were very upset with me because I had been gone

for so long. "Just come home," they said. Once I got back on my feet, I went back to New York and started singing with The Toys again. I left The Toys in 1988 to join Larry Marshacks's Marvelettes.

As I said, I never wanted to go back to drugs again. But I did. I was devastated and depressed when my Mom died in 1996. Mom had always been the strong one, and we thought she would outlive us all. By 1997, I was pulled right back into it, slowly, over many months. It gave me an "up" attitude. Eventually, I started making and smoking crack. Not only was I indulging, but I was also now selling drugs. I didn't see anything wrong with what I was doing, because I was making money. I spent every day using and selling. I was locked in. I was in the worst state of mind in my entire life—and I didn't think I would ever get out. It was like an epidemic. Crack takes everyone over.

By 2000, my family realized that I needed help. My nephew, Robert Dunn, who was a brilliant attorney who covered the O.J. Simpson trial for one of the television networks, came to me and said, "June, I think you should get into a program for a year." I said, "Why do I need a whole year?" Well, once I got into the program, I ended up staying there for 15 months! I was getting three meals a day. I was going to the gym. I was doing the orientation programs for new patients. I was facilitating classes. Singing on the weekends. I felt protected. I finally had some discipline in my life. There hadn't been any discipline since my father died. After Dad died, my brothers took over, and they had problems with me. All I wanted to do was sing. I didn't want to do my school work. Didn't want to do chores. So the program put that discipline back into my life. Every day was productive, and every day was positive. Even if I hadn't had an addiction problem, this would have been good for me! (Robert died in 2006, the same year I discovered I had throat cancer.)

In fact, this was GREAT for me! This was the life. I loved what was going on there. It was a very positive environment. I had the freedom to come and go as I pleased. It was fabulous. Why would I want to go back out there?

Then they told me that I had to leave. They literally had to kick me out of the program! "Please," I said, "you are throwing me to the wolves." They asked me if I wanted to become a counselor. "No," I said, "that would require too much paperwork. What else can I do?" And they said, "June, go back to what you really love doing—singing."

While I was in the program, I had met three great guys—Alan, Teddy and Ricky—and we formed the a cappella group Classic Soul. We got a lot of gigs through others in the industry who heard us at private parties and told others about us. We started performing at fundraisers. We went to New Orleans to perform. And the people who ran the program started getting me motivational speaking engagements. I was making money again, so I was able to get my teeth—which had been destroyed by the drugs—fixed. I didn't even care that Barbara Harris was performing with two other singers as The Toys, and that Barbara Parritt was singing as part of Johnny and Joe. I then went on to be certified by the New York Department of Public Health to give talks about HIV, STDs, and hepatitis prevention. I started doing motivational programs with Classic Soul—"Entertainment with a Message"—at schools, health centers and community centers. God really was using me not just to sing, but to spread the message about the importance of HIV testing. My life had meaning again, and I knew I was going to be OK.

So when I was diagnosed with throat cancer in 2006, the world stopped for me. I flashed back to those happy days as a child, singing with my Dad. I thought I couldn't accomplish my goals. "Oh, my gosh," I thought. "I'm not going to be able to sing any more." Now, I couldn't sing or deliver my message. That's when the fear set in. It wasn't until later that I learned, through my prosperity classes, that F.E.A.R. = False Evidence Appearing Real. Once you let fear into your life, it blocks all goodness and pollutes your mind. All you can think of is being upset and depressed. It was all negative.

Just because I had cancer didn't mean that I couldn't fix it. It didn't have to mean the end of my career. My doctor told me that I would need surgery, and I said, "Listen, I'm a singer. I want the chief surgeon." I knew what had happened to Julie Andrews, who had lost her voice after she'd had surgery, and I didn't want that to happen to me. I told myself, "You are not going to be upset by this. You <u>will</u> have the chief surgeon. And you <u>will</u> sing again!"

Two weeks after my surgery, the cancer was back. My doctor told me that I had to have radiation treatments. Once again, I told myself, "I know I will be OK." During the radiation treatments, I couldn't speak for weeks. I had to write everything down. I went to stay with my sister, and she took care of me. After the treatments were over, I had to learn to talk again—and to sing again! It took a year, and it was a very expensive process. I was working with a wonderful vocal coach—Miss Abigail—but her lessons cost $50 an hour, and I could not afford that on a regular basis. Miss Abigail said, "I think I can help you with half hour lessons." And she did!

When my life was threatened, I prayed and became extremely spiritual. I decided that I wanted to do something with my life—something that really means something. I used to sell drugs—look at how many people's lives I have ruined. I carried that around with me. I had shaken hands with the devil. Could God ever forgive me? That's when I joined the Spiritual Center for Creative Living—the Unity Church. All that negativity, the drugs, the drinking, had no place in my life any more. I started thinking clearly for the first time in a long time. I realized that I could have goodness in my life. I let go and let God take control of my life— I am the power of God in action.

I started singing again with a group called The Hearts, and I am still singing with them. And now, as I am writing this, Barbara Harris, Barbara Perritt and I are re-forming The Toys. I am very excited about our being back together again. This time it will be on a totally different level. The show we are putting together won't be your average, run-of-the-mill production. It will be more auto-biographical, and about how happy we are to be back together. I have come up with two show concepts for the group—"Celebrate Your Life," and "What About Now?" I will also play the flute during our shows, something I haven't done in years!

I still have so many dreams. I sing with Louise Murray and The Hearts (whose big hit was "Lonely Nights"), as well as with The Jaynettes ("Sally Go Round The Roses," Louise Murray also was a member of The Jaynettes). I am a distributor for a food seasoning called, "Ole Man's Rub," based in New Orleans. I will excel in my distribution business. I had written several songs for Pat Pope's play, "Where Black Folks Live," years ago. Recently, I ran into Eugene Pitt, of The Jive Five singing group, when The Hearts were performing on the same show with his group. Eugene told me that The Jive Five are getting ready to record a gospel CD. I said, "Hey, I wrote two gospel songs. Maybe you'd like to hear them?" "Sure," Eugene said. And we are going to record my songs and include them on the CD!

I didn't realize that I am as strong as I am until I went to the Unity Church. I say a lot of affirmations throughout the day. "I am open and receptive to God's living spirit of truth," is one that I say a lot. Nothing negative can ever enter your mind if you say positive affirmations. Have an "attitude of gratitude." Be thankful for what you DO have, and all the rest will be added to your life. In this way, you will always be in the flow of goodness. Whatever you ask for will be given to you. If you focus on your limitations, you will receive limitations. But if you focus on an abundant and limitless life, you will receive an abundant and unlimited life. Wherever you are receiving your spiritual nourishment, tithe there. I am not talking only about money. Give of yourself. Help others. Do something to make a difference in someone's life. What goes around, comes around—what you give, you will receive back in abundance. One of the most positive things I can say to you is to let go, and let God be God in your life.

If I can continue to do the things that are mine to do, I will be OK.

C H A P T E R   9
Korey's Courage
Korene Mosher

Korey Mosher experienced more as a child than many adults would be able to handle, when cancer ravaged her body. Through positive thinking, persistence—and incredible courage—she survived, going on to become an oncology nurse and researcher in adulthood. In the fall of 2013, Korey will enter medical school at Yale University.

Here is how Korey tells her story:

I was 12 years old, sitting by myself in the waiting room of my doctor's office, in my school uniform, while my parents were taken into a private room. I was waiting to get back to school after having some x-rays taken. My parents were learning that my femur bone—I quickly learned its proper name—had been destroyed by cancer, which had invaded the full thickness of the bone and surrounding muscle. I didn't understand. I knew cancer was deadly. I knew they had to remove this bone. They said things like, "reconstructive surgery," "cadaver bones," "rescue drugs," "chemotherapy," "50/50 chance," and many other terms and phrases which I later learned would become the new normal in my life.

That day, I had no idea what to expect, what to plan, or even to have a life dream. I thought I was going to die. My treatment would be over the course of a year or so, and I would be very sick during that year. This, I thought, was my destiny and my future— to live, to suffer, to die. My goals and dreams at 12 turned into making it through the next day. I thought I had no future beyond tomorrow, and that if I could just get through each day, that would be another day I would get to see my family. My isolated world of the Pediatric Oncology Unit 7-2 at the hospital became my home, my life, my community, my friends, my all. At that time, I thought, this was a trial that was larger than life—my roadblock. Maybe my end.

With each new day came new hope that today would be better than yesterday. It had to be, because I woke up. Many nights, I went to sleep thinking that I would not wake up in the morning. When morning came and I woke up, I wanted to make that new day worth it with smiles and fun. I was very sick with toxic and concentrated chemotherapy pumping through my little body. At times, I would stop breathing and black out, and my mother would yell at me to breathe. Many nights, my mother slept by my side at the hospital, just to tell my subconscious mind to take another breathe.

It seemed as if it happened overnight that I went from being an active, adventure seeking, outdoor playing 12 year old, to a very sick and very scared—and very isolated—cancer patient. The active adventure seeker within me did not fade away with the cancer, but took on a new challenge—to go, to be, to do, and to overcome.

I learned to deal with what was going on mentally with thankfulness, and physically by escaping my body. Emotionally, I shut down. I saw my family suffer as they watched me suffer. I decided I was not going to contribute to my perception of their suffering with my own emotional confusion, and overwhelming sense of fear, terror, and torture. So I suffered in silence, and put on a face of strength, endurance, and a false sense of courage. Sure—I was willing to face anything that came my way. But, silently, I was terrified. I discovered that when our physical, mental, and emotional worlds collapse, our spirit rises up and—if fed life—will thrive and carry us forward physically, mentally, emotionally.

At this young age, when my body was near death, my mind was unable to comprehend, and my emotions were shut down, my spirit took over and became my best friend, mentor, comforter, healer, cornerstone, provider, life breathe, and much more. It became God. The hours, days and months that I spent in one bed, in one hospital room, became my sanctuary of peace, joy, hope, and thankfulness. This was when I learned the power and importance of the human spirit, which is nourished by what we think, see, hear, and speak. One life lesson that carried me through these hard times was that we can choose what we feed our spirit—life or death—so be wise in what you bring into your world. Choose what you see, watch and listen to, and what you feed your spirit, because when everything you know collapses, your spirit will carry you through, and will live according to what you feed it.

Over the course of 16 months of primarily inpatient chemotherapy, I watched friends I'd made pass away from various cancers, thinking that each day was my last until my very last treatment. I was confused by the thought of finishing my last round of chemotherapy. I thought I wasn't supposed to make it to the end of—at that time—the experimental protocol. All my friends were gone. But I was still on Unit 7-2, nearing the end of perpetual sickness. I was excited and scared at the same time. I had questions like, how will I return to the outside world, knowing that my real world had become that Pediatric Oncology Unit 7-2?

I was leaving my home, a major part of my life—my warped sense of safety.

Somehow, I had to return to school, which had jumped forward two years—and with a newly reconstructed left leg that I was unable to walk on. I did not know how to move forward other than the same way I had in the hospital—one day at a time, and still suffering in silence the tremendous pain of orthopedic surgeries over and over again, in an attempt to rebuild my left leg, from which two-thirds of the femur bone had been removed.

I dealt with what was going on by being thankful that I was alive and no longer had cancer. The cancer was gone, and now I had this leg that had a bone transplant, but which broke over the course of five years or so. So another bone transplant was attempted and again failed a few years later.

It was then decided that a metal prosthesis was the next option, which would include a total knee replacement, and replacement of most of the femur. I didn't understand the implications of having an internal prosthesis, but I was a teenager determined to finish high school and get my drivers license. I did much of high school at home, because my leg was too fragile and unstable to be in the crowded halls of our high school.

I found swimming at the local pool helpful on so many levels. Being physically active despite my physical limitations was the very thing that my surgeon later said enabled me to walk again. I taught myself how to swim and began swimming laps almost every day.

When I was finally able to attend my local high school for a year and a half, I was accepted onto the swim team. I am not sure if my acceptance was because my older sister had gone through the same school two years ahead of me and knew the coach well, or if I had some competitive lap times.

Either way, it kept me physically active and provided physical therapy, which further rehabilitated my total knee and partial femur replacement. My determination for physical health and to walk normally again was what got me through my high school years. It also brought great triumph into my life over many torturous surgical procedures in an attempt to rebuild my left leg.

The active teenager and adventure seeker in me did not stop at the pool. In between surgeries and years of rehabilitation, I pursued my dream of mountain climbing—which was fueled by a fellow cancer patient. I went on to hike and backpack through the White Mountains and the mountains of Haiti. I found great strength in the mountains, and found that I could not go for very long without a backtracking trip. I discovered that all things are possible with the right supportive equipment and gear. Though I could climb a mountain, I was unable to hike back down all in one day. So most trips lasted a few days.

As an active teenager, I also found interest in dirt bikes and four wheelers. My zeal for outdoor adventure and motorized sports grew with the physical limitations that I had. What I really wanted to do was run, but I couldn't. I felt that the next best thing was to sit on something that could go very fast. The motorized sports lasted a few years, until I decided that riding on the ground wasn't adventurous enough. It was time to do jumps!

Needless-to-say, I crashed one too many times and broke my leg. The leg that had been rebuilt. The leg that gave me a second chance at life. This time, though, I had a better story to tell curious spectators who saw me on crutches in the grocery store, or in a wheelchair at the amusement park. I no longer had to explain that cancer had eaten away my bone. I could now simply state, "Four wheeler accident." And that was the honest truth! My life became simpler in some ways, and more complicated in other ways. This latest break resulted in another reconstruction of my left leg, this time with stainless steel instead of cadaver bone.

Going through an old suitcase in the attic of my parents' house one evening, I found a storybook that I had written about my life when I was about 6 years old. One of the questions in this futuristic storybook was, "What do you want to be when you grow up?" I had written, "a nurse." After the day I thought I might never see—high school graduation—I took a year to find the right nursing school, and ultimately graduated with my bachelor's degree in nursing. The majority of my surgeries and reconstructions were over, or so I thought.

I jumped right into oncology nursing and loved it! All of my personal experience as an oncology patient enabled me to connect with, and experience life with, my patients. At this time in my life—in the middle of a great nursing career—I dealt with my own pains and struggles as a cancer survivor with physical limitations by seeing the impact my life was having on my patients and their family members.

It was then that I realized I have something to share. That very part of my life that was so painful, so potentially destructive, was the very part of my life that now delivered life to those dealing with the same or a similar disease. Seeing this transfer of life made all that I went through worthwhile. And I found smiles, laughs, encouragement, and courage in those I walked with—and sometimes held as they took their last breath. My pain and suffering had turned into meaning, and strength, and life.

What helped me, and continues to help me, triumph over my physical limitations is seeing and experiencing the encouragement, motivation, and inspiration that overcoming my struggles and trials bring to other people's lives. I am so thankful that my life is inspiring to others. If something as terrible as cancer can be used to help someone else get through something in their life, then it is worth finding the way to navigate life with what we have to work with. What was meant for death and destruction is being used for health, and life, and good.

My life is a continual learning process. We are all on this journey together, and we are never alone. My reconstructed leg has a tendency to break or fall apart every few years, leaving me in tremendous pain and needing some major reconstructive, limb sparing, surgical procedure. In fact, I am in the middle of one right now. But daily, I find the strength and wisdom to navigate each day, and to make each day meaningful and productive.

God continues to be the center of my life, and the breath and life in my spirit that rises above everything that tries to bring me down. I surprise myself with my unfailing pursuit of my life dreams and goals. As a teenager, I was fascinated with naturopathic medicine, and am now pursuing that dream of becoming a naturopathic physician. I will begin my medical studies at Yale Medical School in the fall of 2013. Regardless of the condition of my leg, or my ability to walk, I know that I can always help other people reach their optimal level of health and well-being as a naturopathic physician.

Throughout my life, I have learned to love people, to love life, to love health, and to pursue my career goals regardless of the circumstances of my life. I am using these lessons to make a difference in others' lives.

Success for me is not measured by what can be seen, but by what is unseen. It is not a fancy car, or big house, or nice boat. It is the legacy I leave behind. The life breathed into a heart. The smile in the soul of one who feels no reason to smile. The joy found in the spirit of a wonderful soul. The laughter of a child who has no family. When you see life in a person who would seem to have no reason to live. To overcome is to live, and to live free, with abundant peace and joy. Life comes from within. When life is lacking, hope is lacking. And when hope is lacking, faith is lacking. I really believe that in the end all things end right, as in the end of our trials and sufferings.

I like this quote from Charles R. Swindoll: "In the midst of struggles and the storms and the sufferings of life, we can advance our thoughts beyond today and see relief...triumph...victory. Because, in the end, God does, indeed, win."

"Amazing Man"
Glenn Nazarian

Glenn Nazarian is the owner of Danvers (MA)-based Boston North Fitness Center. Prior to starting the Center, Glenn owned 14 Get in Shape for Women Fitness Centers, and was the most successful owner in the franchise. A former car industry executive, Glenn was involved in a life-threatening accident when a drunk driver pushed his car off the road and into a tree. He would spend the next six months of his life in hospitals and rehabilitation centers.

Glenn shares his incredible story:

I should not be alive today. But, let's begin at the beginning of the story.

In 2003, I was 43 years old and the general manager for a large auto dealership—and very out of shape. Due to my work schedule, I did not eat meals on a regular schedule, did a lot of snacking. My weight ballooned to 258 pounds.

One day, I dropped a pencil and, as I bent over to pick it up, I strained my back. I knew it was time to do something. I set a goal to lose 100 pounds within the next year. As an incentive to reach my goal, my children entered me in a body building competition. I didn't want to do it—they had to force me to. I didn't want to parade around in that skimpy swimsuit.

Well, by the time the Cape Cod Classic body building competition rolled around in 2004, I had lost 112 pounds and was in the best shape of my life. Bill Murphy had coached me. I felt good about myself, like I had accomplished something and was becoming successful again. I was hooked. One year later, I won my first competition.

And then it happened....

On my way home to New Hampshire from a competition, all I could think of was having a "cheat meal" of donuts and bagels to celebrate. Out of nowhere, a car slammed into mine and shoved me off the road and into a tree. The guy never stopped. . I don't know if he was drunk or on his cell phone, and to this day we still do not know the driver's identity.

I was rushed to the hospital in critical condition. My leg was practically severed, and the doctors wanted to amputate. I needed 200 stitches in my head, and had nine pins inserted in my shattered heel. I needed multiple skin grafts. I had the same medical team that worked on former Boston Red Sox pitcher Curt Shilling.

The surgeons were able to reattach my leg. My car sustained $50,000 in damage. The first thing I said when I woke up after the accident was, "Will I ever body build again?' My doctor said, "Let's get you out of the hospital first!" I spent the next six months in the hospital and in rehabilitation facilities. I couldn't believe it when I gained back over 50 pounds of the weight I had lost. Even worse, though, I simply could not understand how that other driver could leave me there to die.

It took me a full year to recover—although I will never be fully recovered. I was dubbed the "Amazing Man." And I went back to body building. I lost the weight again. I trained. In fact, in 2012, I finally received my certification as a professional body builder.

That accident was the worst and the best thing that's ever happened to me. When I was ready to go back to work, I was offered another job in the auto industry, at a higher salary than my previous job. But since the accident, I was in chronic pain. I realized that I wanted to do something worthwhile with my life— to use my life and my experience to make a difference in others' lives. Of course, as a body builder, I had spent a lot of time in gyms. After I recovered, I met exercise physiologist Brian Cook, who owned a personalized training studio, online. Brian wanted to franchise his studio, and I wanted to own a gym franchise. It was a match made in heaven! This was a huge risk for me, though. This was a new franchise with no track record. I became the first franchise owner in 2007. My original plan was to open franchises in 4 to 6 locations. Within 13 months, I owned 4 franchises, and that first franchise was to become the biggest in the country. Within 36 months, I owned 16 franchises in three states, representing 30% of the company.

My sister, Robin—who was the best salesperson in the organization—helped me a lot in the beginning as I was buying stores. I wanted people to use our product and to get results. 2000 clients came in. We saw a 200% increase in sales, and Get in Shape for Women became the 66th fastest-growing franchise in the country. This was a life changing opportunity for me, and well worth the risk. My former life had almost killed me.

But I wanted to do even more. When the opportunity presented itself, I sold all but two of my Get in Shape for Women locations and bought Boston North Fitness seven months ago. We completely transformed the facility. And the business is growing by leaps and bounds. We are adding a wellness center. I wanted to bring that "small box" experience to the "big box."

I am asked all the time what is my secret to success. It is

simple. We hire people who care. Some people do their job. Other people care about their job. We hire people who care. I don't own a gym. I change people's lives. It is not necessarily about the results you get physically. It is about the emotional and spiritual results—your self-image and how you feel about yourself.

When you almost lose your life, you begin to see the world differently. I am a lot different now. I have learned so much about myself. There has been a real shift in my energy. The three most important things in life are: 1) your health; 2) your family; and 3) your job—in that order. Yes, there are sacrifices. But you do it.

I often think back to when I joined the hockey team in college. I wasn't the best player—far from it. But I remember the coach saying, "What Glenn lacks in ability, he makes up for in heart and desire." The will to be great comes from heart and desire. It has very little to do with actual ability. It is important how people look at me now. Rather than just doing it, I want to make a difference. I have a lot of "WOW" in my life now! I struck gold doing what I love to do. It is not about the money. It is about making that difference

When I tell my story, it brings back so many memories. I am living proof that if you DO believe—and if you are willing to work hard—you can do anything. You will get there. You can do anything you want—and succeed—if you believe that the glass is half full, not half empty. If you truly believe that you can do something, you will achieve it, if you never look back. We are nothing if we don't truly believe we can do it. It is all about determination and passion. You have to want it. You have to dedicate your life to it. My desire to succeed is because of what I went through—the weight loss, the accident. I am dedicated to the gym. I am dedicated to my employees. I am dedicated to health and fitness.

The journey is important, not just winning. I am very emotional about the journey I have been on—all of it. And I am very appreciative of everything everyone has done for me. It just keeps getting better and better.

The bottom line is, be more appreciative of the things that you DO have in your life. The rest will follow. Keep on persevering. It WILL happen.

Look at me—I am just an ordinary guy doing some pretty amazing things! I should be dead, and I just started living.

Always Have A Goal In Mind
Reed Nixon

In April 1995—at age 17—Reed Nixon, three of his siblings and four of their friends, were involved in a terrible car accident. Reed and his younger brother, Rob, were seriously injured, requiring six months in the hospital and a rehabilitation facility. Their lives—and the lives of their entire family—were changed that day. Reed's mother, Sheryl, wrote a book about her journey of learning to cope with extremely difficult circumstances for which she felt she had no preparation, "In The Blink of An Eye: The Reed and Rob Nixon Story."

Reed's story of healing and hope:

I was born in Provo, Utah, in 1978. My family moved to Texas in 1989. Then we moved to Massachusetts in 1993, when I was 15 years old. We have a very close family, and I have three sisters and two brothers. I had a fairly typical childhood, and loved playing sports and being outdoors. I loved hiking and playing tennis, football and basketball. I attended Algonquin Regional

High School, in Northborough, Massachusetts, and was on the cross-country and track teams.

All that changed on April 4, 1995, when the van I was driving home from a church meeting flipped over on Route 20. There were eight of us in the van—me, my brothers Rob and Kent, my sister Natalie, and four of our friends. Rob was in the front seat with me, and we had our seatbelts on. We broke our necks and suffered spinal cord injuries from the force of the crash. The other six passengers were in the back seats and didn't have seatbelts on. Natalie suffered a bad neck injury. But the other five—including Kent—suffered only minor injuries and walked away from the accident.

Rob and I were life-flighted to the University of Massachusetts Medical Center, where we were admitted to the Pediatric Intensive Care Unit. Initially, my spinal cord injury was at the fourth cervical vertebrae—or C4—the fourth vertebrae down from the head. I also had collapsed lungs and a bruised heart, but I had no head injuries, or any visible outward injuries. However, the doctors had trouble stabilizing my neck, and my condition worsened to a functional spinal cord injury of a level C1-2. I was now a quadriplegic, on a respirator, and had no feeling from my neck down. Rob was not as severely injured as I was. His injury was a level C5-6. But he would still need to spend his life in a wheelchair as a quadriplegic.

After three weeks in the ICU, it was time for Rob and me to move to a rehabilitation facility, to begin the process of learning how to live life in a wheelchair, as well as day-to-day functions. Finding a rehabilitation facility that would take both of us proved more difficult than we thought. Due to the possibility for an accidental mix-up of our medications since we were both "R. Nixon," our parents couldn't find a facility that would take both Rob and me. The only place that would take us both was the Veteran's Administration Hospital (VA), in West Roxbury, Massachusetts. That is where we spent the next six months of our lives. This turned out to be an excellent experience for me, and provided me with a good foundation for learning how to live my life again.

As it grew closer to the time we would be released from rehab, our family realized that our house would need to be totally refitted to accommodate Rob and me. All the bedrooms and bathrooms were on the second floor. Five contractors in our town joined together to build an 1,100 square foot, handicapped-accessible addition to the back of our family home. At about the same time, a man who was dying of cancer gave my parents his handicapped-accessible van.

Once we returned home, Rob and I went back to Algonquin Regional High School. I was in my senior year, and Rob was a junior. But I spent only two or three weeks at the actual high school, because in February of 1996, I developed kidney stones and a bladder infection, and was back in the hospital. I had to finish the rest of my education in the hospital and at home, with tutors. All the changes of coming home and then returning to the hospital, and then back home again, was quite an adjustment—not only for Rob and me, but for our whole family. Sometimes, just the comfort of my family or sitting in my wheelchair next to Rob was a big help in getting through the rough patches. Rob and I kept each other going, because we were experiencing similar frustrations.

The other big factor that helped me—and my whole family—through this traumatic time was our faith. We are members of the Church of Jesus Christ of Latter-Day Saints. Our faith is very important to us. I realized that the Lord was in control of everything. And maybe the Lord had a bigger plan for me. I understood that if I became disappointed or frustrated in the progress I was making, all that did was make other people feel bad. And so I decided, as much as possible, to ponder on my own when I was troubled. If I was able to resolve things on my own, then I would. I knew that some things were unchangeable, but I wanted to resolve as much as possible to my own satisfaction.

Rob and I had set a lot of goals for ourselves before the accident—some of them big, some of them small. Due to our limitations, there were some goals that we could no longer accomplish—like playing sports. But there were a lot of goals that we COULD achieve. We both graduated from high school. We earned our Eagle Scout awards within the scouting program. I had begun my Eagle Scout project before the accident, and I continued with that same project after the accident. And both Rob and I wanted to go to college.

Our Dad is on the faculty at Bentley University, in Waltham, Massachusetts, where he teaches federal tax accounting within the Accounting Department, and so we were eligible to attend tuition-free. After graduating from Algonquin, I enrolled at Bentley as a part-time student, earning my degree in finance, with a minor in history after 10 years. After he graduated from Algonquin, Rob also enrolled at Bentley part-time.

Belonging to the Church of Jesus Christ of the Latter-Day Saints, another one of Rob's goals was to serve a mission for the church. So, after three semesters at Bentley, Rob decided it was time to embark on his church mission. Originally, he was assigned to work one year in the Boston Mission office, so that he could live at home. However, the Mission President wanted Rob to have a regular proselytizing experience. And so, for the first time in his life, Rob lived away from home. After the first year was completed, Rob extended his mission for a second year. It was an amazing, life-changing experience for him. People he met during those two years still remember Rob. After he finished his mission, Rob enrolled at Brigham Young University, where he earned his undergraduate and Master's degrees in accounting. Dad says the apple didn't fall far from the tree! Once he earned his bachelor's and master's degrees at Brigham Young University, Rob moved to California, where he completed his CPA certificate. He is married now, and works as a tax manager at BDO USA, LLP.

My health hasn't been the best, and so after college it wasn't possible for me to have a regular job. But that doesn't mean that I am wasting time sitting around doing nothing. I have always been busy, and inconsistent health wasn't going to stop me. I have an eBay store where I sell sports memorabilia and other sports items.

Several times a year, I speak to third-year medical students during an interclerkship at the University of Massachusetts Medical School. I am able to share my perspective on patient/doctor relations with the students. I help them think outside of the box, finding ways to diagnose illness in non-typical patients like myself. I speak to a law class at Bentley University several times a year, discussing the impact and importance of the Americans with Disabilities Act. I am able to give some personal examples of how it has helped or not helped me. I also regularly speak with high school anatomy and physiology classes about the spinal chord and nervous system, and how the body adapts to traumatic injuries. I am also pleased to be a motivational and public speaker. My motivational speaking engagements focus on getting through the hard times—and how I have dealt with hard times myself.

My family loves to travel, and with their help, I have been able to travel to 25 states and Canada since my injury. In fact, I did the interview for this book while we were on a cross-country trip from Massachusetts to Missouri, Illinois, Kansas, and Iowa. Mom never wanted us to be stuck at home. She wanted us to see and experience as much as possible even though it took a lot of planning and a lot of work.

It's not always easy. In fact, it's never easy. But I just haven't let my disability stop my life or prevent me from having fun. Even though I am not able to participate physically in sports any longer. But I can still be a fan. I can be a coach. I can inspire others. Maybe it's not exactly as it was before my accident, but I can still find a way to participate and have fun. If something is important enough to you, you WILL find the way to work it out.

Even though my physical circumstances have changed, I am

still able to enjoy life—and there is a lot to enjoy. There are a lot of fun things to do and to experience. We should always have a goal in mind—whether big or small. We may not always achieve our goals but striving for a goal—striving for excellence—helps to keep us focused. It helps us to get over the "woe is me" rut. It helps us to avoid getting stuck in sadness. My goal is to use my disability to help society—to make a difference in the world. When we serve others, we forget many of our own problems. It really changes your attitude and your motivation.

I am hopeful—always—for what the future may bring. Maybe I can't change my physical situation, but I CAN still choose to be positive and happy!

∽

Take A Look and Let It Go
Corrie Painter

Corrie Painter is a wife, mother and biomedical researcher at the University of Massachusetts Medical School. In 2010, she was diagnosed with primary angiosarcoma of the breast—an extremely rare and insidious disease that affects only about 300 people per year, and has a dismal survival rate.

Three years after her diagnosis and treatment, Corrie is cancer-free and shares her story here:

In February of 2010, I found a lump in my breast. I thought the worst-case scenario was that I had breast cancer. Best case was that I had a lot of resources at my disposal. I went for diagnostic tests at the University of Massachusetts Medical Center, and my doctor told me that it wasn't breast cancer. He had a report that indicated I had angiosarcoma, which is an incredibly rare form of cancer. He didn't believe the report, and wanted to send me to Dana-Farber Cancer Institute to get some experts involved my case. I went to Dana-Farber still not sure what my diagnosis was. They did 10 biopsies, straight through the tumor. "We don't think you have angiosarcoma, but we'll still take out the lump so you don't have to worry about it," I was told. On May 20, I went in for a routine lumpectomy. When I woke up from surgery, I had a partial mastectomy because, as I was told by the surgeon, "It looked really ugly, and I've never seen anything that ugly that wasn't malignant." The breast tissue was sent to pathology for testing.

A week later, I still hadn't received any test results. I called Dana-Farber and was told it was definitely intermediate-grade angiosarcoma.

Time is relative, depending on what stage of life you are at. My whole sense of timing throughout this process was so full of gravity. Time was weighing so heavily on me, and I was not even sure where in time I was.

After it was confirmed that I had angiosarcoma, I was scheduled for a radical mastectomy, with this second surgery intended to get the clean margins they needed. Then, it was a matter of what kind of follow-up treatment I would receive.

This was so rare—there are only about 300 cases of angiosarcoma diagnosed worldwide each year. My medical team wasn't sure what the next step should be. They had no idea how to treat me. So, they looked at me and said, "What do you want to do?" To which I responded, "What do you recommend?" "We don't really know because there are aren't enough people who get this."

Now, as a scientist, this threw me into a tailspin! So I tried to find the answers. I looked all over the place—Memorial Sloan-Kettering, UMass, wherever there were experts. Ultimately, I decided to do a few rounds of chemotherapy, but to stop before having any serious side effects, so that if the cancer came back, I could use that same chemotherapy treatment again. At that point, the prognosis was still so grim. Because so few people survive angiosarcoma, the experts just don't know what the long-term outlook is.

I am 3 years out from my surgery, and still cancer-free. But I know it could come back at any time. I live day-to-day knowing that. I'm fine and there is no evidence of the disease, but every bruise, every pain, every headache, every sore throat, every sneeze, could signal a recurrence. One of the biggest obstacles I have is overcoming that sense of impending doom with every single little thing.

Really, though, I still don't have any real fear of dying. I truly don't. I have complete peace with the thought of not being alive. In terms of my life, I have done all that I could do, and then some—and did it successfully. There is nothing left for me to accomplish, no "golden ring" that I have to snatch before I die. I don't need to live to do one more thing.

When I was diagnosed, my first thoughts were for my children. How do I look at them, so young and innocent. Those were very tough times for me. Now, I only live for my children, because I want to raise them to be strong and happy, whatever direction that takes them in. I know that being here will help me to direct them—to get to those goals they want to accomplish.

I decided immediately that I have no control over this disease, other than trying to stay as healthy as I can. What I DO have control over is my reaction to it. Even if this disease takes me out in a month, I have that month, every second of it. If I am in physical pain, I don't have to shout out. If I am in psychological pain, I don't have to cry. I can learn how to take it. I can take those challenges and turn them into strengths. And by those methods, I can take those situations and turn them into life lessons for my children.

How did I do it? I decided right from the start that, if I am going to have cancer and if I'm going to be bald, we are going to have some fun with it. So we had shaving cream contests. Each girl would take one side of my bald head and see who could make the silliest thing on it with shaving cream. I bought stick-on rhinestones and let them spell things out with them—and then we went out in public to see people's reactions. I bought the most ridiculous wigs and wore them in public for fun. In these ways, I took a completely devastating reality and made it so it wasn't so scary for them.

I demystified my disease for them. They weren't embarrassed by it. My natural inclination was to be upbeat and positive, and to have as much fun with my babies as possible. I keep a blog, so that when they grow up, they will know my thoughts and feelings. They will be able to reflect back and say, "WOW! She was dying and she had a smile on her face. If she could do that, I can do anything!"

It was still very painful, though. But it was never a choice to give in. I intrinsically know who I am. I looked at my children and said, "There's no other option." Every parent wants to be the best parent for their children. The best thing for them is for me not to give in to pain, and fear, and depression. I don't know if there's a source I tapped into for that, other than my love for my children.

My daughters were two and four when I was diagnosed, so they had no concept of mortality. That's why I chose to do it the way I did. We didn't talk a lot about life and death. What are they going to see? They're going to see Mommy be bald. They're going to see Mommy with one breast. How do I make that not scary for them? That's why I went the tack of silly.

They would ask questions, and I would say, "My breast was sick, so the doctors had to take it off," and, "in order to keep from being sick, I have to take medicine that makes my hair fall out."

My little one is five now, and my older daughter is eight. They both know the word, angiosarcoma. They hear me talk about it all the time. They see me helping people in our support group, making phone calls, going to meetings.

I am doing research on melanoma so that I can fund research into angiosarcoma. The girls come to my lab sometimes and help me set up my experiments. They understand what cancer is, that it makes you sick. My older daughter knows that Mommy helps other people with angiosarcoma, and that they die all the time.

I use my experience as a lesson every time they face a challenge. To get them to step back from their problem. To see it for what it really is, and to see it from another perspective. To see it as really little. If they can see their problem as being little, they can pick it up in their hands and throw it away.

I want them to see the problem for what it really is in the grand scheme of things. I want them to be in the moment. They don't have to be scared of that math problem. They don't have to feel the anxiety build up inside them, because that math problem isn't hurting them, and it won't embarrass them. They can understand that the math problem is very small in the grand scheme.

You can transform whatever you have learned into any medium you want, and transfer it to someone else undergoing a completely unrelated problem, big or small. The meaning of that lesson is to truly understand yourself and your interpretation of the situation—your understanding of how to go about solving those problems for them.

I was at the tail end of completing my Ph.D. when I was diagnosed. I thought that I might just stay a perpetual graduate student. The thought of writing my thesis, the thought of having to get new insurance, of having to leave the lab I was so comfortable in, and the people I loved—the thought of starting anything new was terrifying. And I think my department and the school probably would have allowed me to stay on without graduating. It was scary to think of change at that time.

But I had to try to find others with my disease, to get their perspective and understanding of what I was going through. They were hard to find, because there were so few of them. I finally found a Facebook group—Angiosarcoma Cancer—started by

Lauren Ryan, who had received the same diagnosis the year before I did. There were three or four others in the group. I became instant soul mates with all of them.

Lauren told me that she had started the paperwork to form a 501(C)3 non-profit organization to help those with angiosarcoma connect with available resources. We met in New York City, and decided that we wanted to form Angiosarcoma Awareness, Inc. Our goal was to raise $10,000 through fundraising that first year, and to use that as seed money to put on bigger fundraisers in the future.

As a biomedical researcher, I knew the harsh reality that you can't really do research with a few thousand dollars. We needed hundreds of thousands—millions—of dollars to make an impact. My mission became to raise the money and, as the scientific officer, to figure out where to put it to get the most bang for our buck.

Within the first couple of months, we raised $40,000. We do fundraising on our own, and have a number of members in our support group who also put on events to bring money into the organization. We also have grateful donors who, even when they die, still want to give. We have formed a partnership with Memorial Sloan-Kettering Cancer Center, by participating in the Cycle for Survival annual fundraiser. Last year, we raised $117,000 with Memorial Sloan-Kettering Cancer Center, and another $100,000 through our own initiatives.

The money raised in partnership with Memorial Sloan-Kettering Cancer Center funds clinical and basic science in labs dedicated to angiosarcoma research at Memorial Sloan Kettering. We can tell the people who raised that money exactly what their money is doing, the papers published, etc. It is a perfectly closed loop. There is no question that they have made an impact with their donations, and that galvanizes people. It's the same with the money that comes in through our own charity. I am in direct contact with the scientists, and am very involved in the whole process.

Our organization, and the fundraising, is wonderful. It's a novel way to conduct and fund research. We help angiosarcoma scientists to collaborate where they might not otherwise. This helps to create synergy within this small field of research.

Our Facebook support group now has over 1000 members—friends, family, and those affected with this disease. It has been transformative. There were so few resources at first. We found the resources. We can now share those resources with the people who need them. We have made the connections with the researchers and the doctors. We can cut through the red tape—our partners are compelled to help us.

We have brought everybody together. We are saving lives by being so quick. We can provide people with the resources they need within a day or two of their diagnosis. Through the support group, we compare notes—who are the best doctors, what are the side effects. Who needs support because they just lost a child. This is an unbelievably tragic disease. It's unbelievable that there's a place to go where people understand. It helps to take the edge off the exquisite pain.

You must be seen by a team of experts as soon after diagnosis as possible. You have to get the proper treatment and follow-up care. Early diagnosis is important.

I was fortunate to have an excellent surgeon at Dana-Farber. He cut out everything and got the clean margins he wanted. There were no malignant cells in the bordering tissue. Now, I do all that I can to stay healthy and clean. I do things because I'm superstitious! I am careful about my diet. I eat raw berries and cinnamon for breakfast, a raw lunch, and olive oil-sauteed vegetables over protein-enriched pasta for dinner. Every day. I drink a lot of green tea. Ultimately, the thing I believe most is that if I am to be cured, the reality is because I had a good surgeon. That's what motivates me to get people to the experts as fast as possible.

Throughout my whole life, I have always been a searcher. I was always looking for the meaning of life. When I was a teenager,

I was a horrible student—but I always read books way beyond my comprehension. I didn't understand them at all. I was searching for things, but I didn't know how to look.

I was always jaded and cynical. One day, when I was in my mid-twenties, I woke up and noticed that my face was distorted. I realized it was anxiety-driven. "This is ridiculous," I thought to myself. "I have absolutely nothing to complain about. It was at that point that I made a conscious decision to visualize myself and whatever problem I'm facing, and take a side-step away from it. My philosophy is, take a look and let it go.

My advice to you, based on my experience? Stop beating yourself up. In fact, stop thinking about yourself so much. Take the time to look at things outside yourself. What does it feel like to be that leaf on the tree? What does it feel like when the wind blows over you? This opened me up to everything else. There's a great big world out there.

Treat yourself like you would treat your best friend. You wouldn't belittle your best friend, would you? Then why belittle yourself?

And when you do engage other people, really engage them. Look in their eyes. Notice their facial expressions. What are they trying to tell you? If you walk away from a conversation only remembering what you said, then you haven't really engaged.

These are all the self-taught things that helped me to over-come my teenage-y angst—the spoiled rotten little problems I thought I had and had to overcome. It has helped me to become less jaded and cynical. It has brought me to a path where I can live in the moment. I want to to suck the marrow out of life! That's why, when I was diagnosed, I was never scared of it. I was already a solid person when I was diagnosed.

Whether you are in a good place in life, or in a bad place, there is always work to be done. So if you are hit with adversity, you are on solid ground. For me, that made all the difference in the world.

So often, when adversity strikes, we just drift with the debris. We swim so hard—up with every wave, and down with every wave. We don't know where we are, because we just drifted along aimlessly. And we're no closer to where we wanted to be in the first place. We latched on to that false sense of security—the debris—and got nowhere.

When I was diagnosed, I was cast out to sea. But, I had a solid mooring. No matter how big the waves got, I knew exactly where I was, and if I just held on, everything would be still and calm again. I knew I would find solid ground.

Don't take life too seriously.

Re-Dream the Dream
Scherrie Payne

Scherrie Payne is a singer, songwriter, and playright. From 1973 to 1977, Scherrie was lead singer of The Supremes, recording three albums with the group. Prior to joining The Supremes, Scherrie sang with the Invictus Records quartet Glass House, for whom she wrote several songs. Her sister, Freda Payne, also has recorded some of Scherrie's compositions. After The Supremes disbanded in 1977, Scherrie recorded a couple of solo singles for Motown as well as a critically acclaimed album, "Partners," with fellow Supremes-alumna Susaye Greene. Scherrie continues to perform today, as a solo artist, as well as part of Former Ladies of The Supremes and jazz quintet Tour De 4Force. One of her plays, "It Always Rains on Sunday,' had its premier in Los Angeles in November, 2012.

Scherrie's story:

The question of facing an insurmountable obstacle is very profound. I am not really sure I would characterize any of the challenges I have faced as being insurmountable. After all, here I am!

From the time I was small, I was a gregarious child. My sister, Freda, was an introvert. I was the extrovert. As a child, Freda would not sing in front of people for anything! If our Mom asked her to sing a song at a party, Freda would sing it from behind the curtains. I, on the other hand, commanded the room! I'd sing my little song and then say, "Do you want to hear it again?" Mom said I was singing before I could talk.

Around the age of 10 or 11, though, our roles reversed. Freda knew at age 11 that she wanted to be a singer. I didn't know what I wanted. I became the introvert. I didn't feel the confidence that I needed to have. I don't know why that changed.

Well, maybe I do know why. About that time, Freda and I were in a talent contest in Detroit. Freda was in the Senior Division, and I was in the Junior Division. Freda won in her division. When I came off the stage, I went over to my father and said, "How did I do, Daddy?" He said, "You didn't sound very good." Little words like that can hurt a child so much, even without knowing it. I never even shared that experience with my sister, or my mother and step-dad.

During that time, too, Mom took me on auditions for local television shows. I was called back for two of them. But something happened every time that prevented Mom from taking me back. The first time, her brother had been diagnosed with tuberculosis. The second time, Mom's mother had died. What was preventing me from moving forward with my dreams?

Mom was a very spiritual person, and she took us to Bethel AME Church in Detroit every Sunday. Diana Ross also attended there. I sometimes wonder why I didn't know Diana back then. We would have been in the same Sunday School class. But I remember that you couldn't do anything on Sundays, like play records, dance, etc. Our mother was very strict about that. As a teenager, I remember thinking, "I am never stepping back inside a church again." I didn't have a good spiritual foundation until I was in my twenties. And I didn't really return to the Lord until 1977, when Mom died.

When Freda graduated from high school, she immediately went on the road with Pearl Bailey. That was the start of her singing career. When I graduated, I wanted to be a pediatrician. I enrolled in the pre-med program at Michigan State University. My Uncle asked what I planned to study. When I told him that I wanted to be a doctor, he said, "You'll never make it." Hurtful and negative words can bring you down. You get depressed. Sometimes you give up.

Eventually, I earned my degree in medical technology, although I never did my internship. I started substitute teaching, and went to Wayne State University to get my teaching certificate. I was always creative, but my creativity seemed to come in phases. First, I was into knitting. Then, while I was at Michigan State, I started painting. I also sang in a group at Michigan State. Then, I started writing songs.

When Brian and Eddie Holland, and Lamont Dozier—the legendary songwriting team of Holland-Dozier-Holland—left Motown in 1968, they formed their own label in Detroit, Invictus Records. When Freda came home after being on the road with Pearl Bailey, she got a call from Eddie Holland, saying that they wanted to offer her a recording contract. While she was on the phone, I started playing the piano and singing…very loudly… and on purpose. Eddie asked Freda, "Who is that?" Freda put me on the phone. Eddie said to me, "Do you want to come in for an audition?" "I don't care," I replied. But I went in and played four or five of my songs at the piano. They signed me to the label the next day. Invictus already had a number of solo singers, so they said they were going to form a group around me and Ty Hunter.

Eventually, Larry Mitchell and Pearl Jones were chosen to complete the group. That was the birth of The Glass House. I loved them. We were a family. We recorded a lot of my songs, including "Crumbs Off the Table," "The Fox," and "Horse and Rider." And Freda recorded one of my songs on her first album. But, I was disheartened when I saw that other names were included in the credits on songs that I had completely written, or my name was put last. I stopped writing songs, because I felt I was being taken advantage of. I guess I was naïve to the business. (Freda went on to have two huge, Top Five hits on Invictus—"Band of Gold" and "Bring The Boys Home," as well as a number of other hits.)

I was dating Lamont Dozier when, in late 1973, Mary Wilson called him to say she was looking for a new member for The Supremes, and did he know anyone. This was a critical time in The Supremes' career, as both Jean Terrell and Lynda Laurence had left the group to start families. Long-time member Cindy Birdsong, who replaced Florence Ballard in 1967 and left the group in 1972 to start her family, had agreed to rejoin The Supremes. But Mary still needed a third member. There were concert dates coming up in Ohio and New Mexico. I flew out to Los Angeles and auditioned for Mary. And, that was it—I was in. Overnight, I became one of The Supremes! My time with The Supremes was a wonderful time in my life. It seems like a fairy tale now—it was so long ago! I had experiences many young ladies never get to have. I traveled all over the world. We taped a television concert special in Japan in 1974. We co-headlined in Las Vegas with Joel Grey. It was an inspirational and blessed time in my life.

But that doesn't mean it was easy. It was over a year before we recorded our first album as a group, due to contractual issues. We were on the road constantly. The group's fortunes had changed, and our records were not selling as well as they used to. Then, early in 1976, Cindy left the group again. Mary hired Susaye Greene to replace Cindy. We thought we had a new start when our 1976 album, "High Energy," entered the *Billboard* album chart at Number 40. At the end of the year, though, Mary announced that she was leaving the group to start her solo career. A few months later, my seven year romance ended.

My mother was diagnosed with breast cancer in 1973. She died on March 20, 1977. I realized how life can be so fleeting, and how much I had taken for granted. I never imagined my life without my mother. I thought I would never recover from her death. It completely devastated me! A part of me died with her and I lost my way for a few years. I allowed some people to just walk over me. I wouldn't speak up for myself. I probably appeared to be weak-minded and somewhat flighty. Maybe I was.

I felt so all alone. The loneliest I've ever felt. Freda was married. I had no one. Nothing. Just a twice-broken heart. I was full of anger and turned my back on God.

Initially, it was decided that Susaye and I would continue the group with a new third member, Joyce Vincent, formerly of Tony Orlando and Dawn. That was not to be. The Supremes performed their final farewell concert at London's Drury Lane Theatre on June 12, 1977—the culmination of an extensive European tour. The concert was broadcast live on BBC Radio. It would be almost two years before Susaye and I released our duo album on Motown, "Partners," for which we wrote all the songs. It was Susaye who encouraged me to start writing again.

Looking back on those days of turmoil for The Supremes and for me, I realize that maybe if I had been more vocal—if I had spoken up for myself and for the group—maybe I could have made a difference in the group's future. I just didn't care about anything at that time.

I was back in the recording studio in the early 1980s, and recorded a number of songs that actually made the charts, including "I'm Not In Love," "One Night Only" (from "Dreamgirls"), "On and On," and "Money Talks" (both duets with Philip Ingram). I sang background on other people's records, and on other people's tours. By the mid-80s, though, I was in a rut again, and not sure where I was going. I wrote two musicals, "10 Good Years" and "DreamSeekers." I wrote all the music for these shows, and even did the recordings at my home. The Originals (another Motown group) recorded some of the background vocals, as did my good friends Jim Gilstrap, and Joyce and Pam Vincent. At about the same time, my daughter's father, Ronnie Phillips of Superstar International Records, formed the group F.L.O.S.— Former Ladies of The Supremes—with me, Jean Terrell (whom I had replaced in The Supremes), and Cindy Birdsong. Lynda Laurence replaced Cindy in F.L.O.S., just as she had replaced Cindy in The Supremes in 1972. Our first record, "We're Back," made the charts. We toured Europe regularly, and recorded several CDs. But by the late 80s, I was starting to lose confidence in myself again. I couldn't sing. I was forgetting lyrics. One Sunday morning in church, I even blanked out on the words to The Lord's Prayer. That's when I started writing screenplays—to compensate for the musical ability I thought I had lost. Over the years, I have written 17 screenplays. I am currently working on my 18th.

I felt like I was just meandering through life, though. Where did the years go? About ten or so years ago, I said, "Hey, I'm in my 50s and I don't know what I want to do!" What was preventing me from moving forward, from reaching my full potential? I realized that my biggest obstacle was ME! I was always getting in my own way. I was afraid to step out of my world, out of my comfort zone. I did only what I needed to get by. Also, I have had a tendency to depression ever since high school. It's like a blanket is covering my head. I used to wallow in it. Even Freda doesn't know this about me. Now, I am able to talk myself out of it. My Mom worked too hard to raise me to let depression control my life.

I was diagnosed with breast cancer in February of 2011. I looked at that mountain and cried for only a brief moment. Then, I prayed. I remembered my faith and I grew stronger and stronger. I evicted Satan and called him a LIAR! This was not going to be a death sentence.

Right before my surgery, my minister was there and as we began to pray, I felt someone take my other hand. It was the surgical nurse, whose name was Grace. After the surgery, I was to have chemotherapy. I told the doctor that I would take the pills for five years, but I was not going to take chemotherapy. Boy, he was SO shocked! I refused the chemotherapy and to this day, I'm doing just great. I see my oncologist every three months to have blood drawn. I go to Cedars-Sinai Hospital every six months for my mammogram and ultra-sound. My next doctor's appointment is in a few weeks—I already know that I am fine!!

And, you know what? We are all human. It's OK if you don't have all the answers. Don't feel isolated, like you are the only one. We all make mistakes. Don't beat yourself up over it. Use it as a learning experience. Pick yourself up and move on. Don't beat yourself over the head. Don't have regrets. That won't change anything. Just go from that point forward. If you don't feel like praying today, it's OK. Try to pray tomorrow.

What have I learned on my life's journey? As I said earlier, I didn't come back to the Lord until my Mom died in 1977. It was Motown producer Frank Wilson—who produced many of The Supremes' hits in the '70s and who passed away just last year—who brought me back to the Lord through his ministry. And I realized that I hadn't been listening to the voice of God. God has your back. It is all a matter of having a strong spiritual foundation. We need that foundation to fall back on—in case you should ever crash. Talking to God has helped me get through the tough times. I talk to God a lot, especially when I am driving. I know that God gave Freda and me this gift to sing. In addition to singing popular music and jazz, I sing in my church. Now, some have chastised me, saying that I shouldn't be singing secular music. I don't agree. God wants me to use His gift for His glory AND to make people happy.

You are going to have good days and bad days. But the bad days don't last. Encourage yourself. Don't give up if you have a dream. Do what brings you joy, even if no one else likes it. Follow your dreams and your passion. Don't let anyone take your dreams from you, or tell you that you can't do something. Even if you do fail, at least you tried. Maybe the best advice I got from my Mom was to always have a Plan B. That's not to say that Plan A won't work. But, plan ahead so that if you do hit a road block, you can get around it.

I love the song, "Here's To Life," by Shirley Horn—"All you give is all you get. So give it all you've got...." Go for it!

Make your dream work. Re-dream your dream.

One of my favorite passages from Scripture comes from Psalm 30—For the night weeping may tarry; with the morning light comes joy.

You see? God has been with me—all the way! Many prayed for me, and their prayers—along with mine—were answered.

I have no regrets.

∽

There Needs To Be One Who Becomes A Catalyst
Annette Rafferty

Born and raised in Worcester, Massachusetts, Annette Rafferty entered the Congregation of the Sisters of St. Joseph, in Springfield, Massachusetts, in 1952 to begin a lifetime commitment to teaching. In 1973, she was invited by the Roman Catholic Diocese of Worcester to coordinate a Task Force on Homeless Women—only to be told later that she was not qualified for the task she had been assigned. Undeterred, and knowing the desperate need for a shelter for women, Annette forged ahead with an amazing group of women, founding Abby's House in 1976. Thirty-seven years later, Abby's House is thriving and growing—and still very much needed—"a bright spot in the city."

Annette's story:

In 1973, I received two invitations. Father Frank Scollen, Director of the Urban Ministry Commission of the Roman Catholic Diocese of Worcester, asked me to coordinate a Task Force on Homeless Women. Because of my deep commitment to finding ways to improve the lives of women, I said "yes" without hesitation.

Shortly thereafter, I was invited by Cameron MacDonald, of the Worcester Ecumenical Council, to join a women's committee looking at the role of Women in Religion and Society. Again, I said yes—and I saw that both groups could play a role in addressing the increasingly pressing needs of homeless women in Worcester. At this time, there was no shelter for women, and few services.

I immersed myself in the work of both groups. Frankly, I found the women's committee to be more supportive. The Urban Ministry Commission, which met monthly, was made up primarily of influential, male church leaders, who were more interested in controlling the meetings. I gave monthly reports, based on the information and statistics I was gathering. Health providers were seeing a need among their female patients. Pastors in the downtrodden Main South section of Worcester were seeing the need for more social services for women.

With each report, though, there was a subtle undermining by the other members of the Commission of the work I was presenting. "You are getting these statistics from so many different places, they are invalid," they said. "You are a wonderful teacher, but you are out of your field here. You are not a social worker." These comments were intended to make me feel inferior. This was still a time when women doing this kind of thing were viewed as workers, not leaders. And, indeed, I did begin to doubt and question myself.

But I kept going. "I have to do this," I said to myself. Eventually, the Commission gave in, and in 1975, agreed to partner with the Ecumenical Council to establish a fund for homeless women, to be called the Abby Kelley Foster Fund (in honor of Worcester's own Abby Kelley Foster, a strong advocate for human rights who herself had experienced homelessness during her life).

Women needing shelter were referred to the YWCA, but the YW soon determined, rightly so, that temporary shelter in their facility wasn't an appropriate fit for their housing program. Finally, in June of 1975, the Commission took a vote on whether or not establishing an emergency shelter for women would be a priority.

I truly thought it would happen, because just the year before, the Commission had taken a stand for gay rights. The vote was "no." I resigned from the Commission immediately. Some asked me to wait, but I said, "I am going to move ahead with this project." As is my way, you only go forward by going forward!

At the same time all this was happening, the Women in Religion and Society Committee WAS moving forward. In 1974, we held a conference at YWCA—"Women's Rites"—which included scripture scholars and theologians. One of the workshops offered the first public presentation of the Abby Kelley Foster Fund, and was perhaps the first time the issue of the need for an emergency shelter for women was presented publicly. The session was packed! Although it would be another two years before it opened, this conference marked the birth of Abby's House.

I realized that if this work was to be done, women had to be the initiators. I found my voice, threw off the patriarchal ways, and found that a small group of people CAN change the world... or at least a small part of it.

Out of the "Women's Rites" conference was born the Women's Collective. Through the remainder of the year, we gathered a group of interested friends and supporters. We met at Holy Cross College. We formed committees. We began a grass roots fund raising campaign. We spoke to any group or organization that would listen to us.

And, we started looking for property,and for grants. We began designing the shelter—it would be open only at night, and there would be no questions asked of the women coming to us for help. We had only $1200 in the bank, but we proceeded as if we were Bill and Melinda Gates! Money—or the lack thereof—was no obstacle for us! The question was not, "shall we establish a shelter?" Our statement was, "We WILL establish an emergency shelter for women!" In February, 1976, we began the process of incorporating as a non-profit—The Abby Kelley Foster House, Inc.

There was one obstacle, though. We had everything else we needed, but we still had no physical location for Abby's House. At our March 30 committee meeting, a woman came for the first time—Carolyn Packard. I am convinced that she embodied the spirit of Abby Kelley Foster herself! Carolyn said, "Have you looked on Crown Street? There's a building there that looks empty." And that's when things really started moving.

On April 4, we found ourselves standing outside 21-23 Crown Street in Worcester. We met the landlord, who was painting the front room at number 21. We told Harry what we were looking for, and what our plans for the space were. We told him that we only had money enough to rent one of the apartments on the number 23 side of the duplex. Harry said, "Oh, but you have to see the upstairs." It was perfect! And he was willing to rent both floors to us for $325—heat and electricity included! We took other committee members to see the building on April 16. Everyone loved it! We were on our way. Our dream was coming true.

The community that got involved in this project after the conference came alive. We continued our grass-roots efforts. In May, we sent out letters to area churches and other organizations, asking for donations of furnishings, dishes, cooking utensils, etc. Within one month, we had everything we needed!

Abby's House opened its doors on June 7, 1976. I had done my job. I was only a part of the whole. But there needs to be one who becomes the catalyst—who pushes, who speaks up and who creates a confidence among the groups that will accomplish the tasks. I learned that I am such a person. I was able to identify leadership among the Collective. I worked well with the other women who had gifts that I lacked. I learned the amazing power of a feminist model—a collective of women—undaunted, having equal decision-making power, and sharing the tasks.

This isn't to say there weren't still ups and downs. We tried to get a block grant from the City of Worcester in 1980, but the City Manager didn't think Abby's House "fit" the criteria for a grant. So we invited members of the City Council to come to Abby's for breakfast. The residents served them and talked with them. "Who are these women, and where did they come from?" the councilors asked. Well, many of our residents were left homeless when the state decided to deinstitutionalize Worcester State Hospital. The City Council sent us a check for $33,000.

Now we had the statistics to show the need for a women's shelter. We wanted to buy the house. We talked to our landlord, and he said that Beacon Corporation was also interested in buying the property, which was now valued at $150,000.

It was to become a parking lot. At about the same time, the Worcester Preservation Society decided that the houses in the Crown Hill section needed to be researched for their historical significance. It was determined that 21-23 Crown Street was indeed an historic building (the Carter-Whitcomb House) and therefore could not be demolished. The Greater Worcester Community Foundation found some funds for us, and we received additional donations. In 1980, we bought the house!

The accomplishments of the previous six years were due to the work of the Worcester community. People came together. It is a testament to what a small group of people can accomplish. Abby's House is a symbol of so much more. A small group of people DOES have the power to change the world!

My story is one of commitment. I made a difference. This represented a major change in my life. When I started out in 1974, I was a Sister of St. Joseph. I left the Congregation in 1986. I decided that Abby's House—and advocating for the needs of women—would need my full-time commitment. I had to make a choice. No one will ever know how hard and sometimes painful it was for me to break the mold of what was, at that time, the stereotypical woman doing what men thought best. Maybe I'm a little like the women in the controversial book, "Lean Forward." And I am definitely like "Rosie the Riveter"—a can do person!

Through it all, I learned that women frighten groups of men. Women doing for women was unheard of at the time! I had always been respectful of authority, but I learned there was a push back in me. Giving up thirty-four years as a religious was a complete letting go. The group gave me the courage. I learned that I have a stubborn streak!

I was lucky to come along at a time when there was relative peace in the world. Abby's still has strong community support and donors, and I still write all the thank you notes to our donors. I have learned more in the last 40 years than if I had gone on to earn my Ph.D. This was the best education of my life.

There is still so much need. Some people just can't pull themselves up by their own bootstraps. I have learned to love a lot of people. I let them find their own answers. I'm a fixer—but I can't do everything.

Today, with the community of people involved, Abby's House has grown into a multiservice organization, providing shelter, housing, advocacy, and supportive services for homeless and abused women, with or without children. From one building, we have grown into four buildings and are the largest provider of housing in the city.

What wisdom do I want to leave with you? Trust your inner feelings and your gut. Keep going forward—but not alone. Find your voice. Be clear and focused about what you want. And don't give up. It may not turn out exactly as you planned, but don't give up.

Every time I reach out for inspiration, I feel the spirit of

Abby Kelley Foster is there. She pointed the way to Crown Street. When Abby's House moved to our new, bigger facility on High Street, I learned that Abby had once lived in a house around the corner, on Chatham Street. You need to nurture your inspiration.

It's been fun.

∾

C H A P T E R   1 5

I Can Do This!

Tom Ingrassia

2009 and 2010 were, perhaps, the darkest times in my life. During an 18-week period between November and March, we lost my father, my mother, and my mother-in-law. We had lost Barbara's father just a year before. My father's death on November 4 came after a four-month hospitalization during which he lost sight in one eye, had a series of infections, and began a rapid descent into dementia, which ended in having to move him into a nursing home. We buried Dad on what would have been my parents' 62nd wedding anniversary.

Both of our mothers died with virtually no warning and no time to prepare ourselves. Barbara's mother was hospitalized for emergency surgery on November 16, when a massive tumor ruptured her bowel. She never regained consciousness following surgery, and died on November 21. Coming so soon after my father's death, our emotions were still raw—and this was like rubbing salt in them. That year, Barbara and I spent both Thanksgiving and Christmas apart—she needing to be with her brother in upstate New York, and me needing to be with my mother in southern New York.

For eight months, from August 2009 to early March 2010, I made almost weekly trips to New York—first helping my mother to attend to my father's medical needs and advocating for him while he was in the hospital and nursing home. (At one point while Dad was hospitalized, I asked his primary care physician what Dad's prognosis was. Within earshot of Mom, he said, "He's old. He's sick. He's going to die. What more do you want me to tell you?") All the while, I also needed to keep my business running, plus I had a very lucrative consulting contract. I was exhausted both physically and emotionally.

Then, without any warning, on March 16, Mom was hospitalized. She hadn't been feeling well for a couple of weeks, and her doctor was treating her for what he felt was a heart problem. It turned out that she had bacterial pneumonia, and by the time they caught it, the infection had already started to spread through her blood system. On March 20, she was transferred to ICU, and I received a phone call that I should get there ASAP. I got to the hospital at about two that afternoon, and spent several hours at Mom's bedside, until her nurse suggested that I go home and get something to eat, while they bathed Mom and got her ready for sleep. When I left the hospital, Mom was in relatively good spirits. Less than two hours later, the hospital called to say that Mom had taken a turn for the worse and that I needed to get back to the hospital immediately—they didn't think she would make it through the night. By the time I got to the hospital—a 15-minute drive from my parents' house—Mom was in a coma. She died at about 11 PM. Until two weeks before, she had been the healthiest of our four parents. We had planned to bring her to Massachusetts to spend a week with us at Easter. And we planned to take her to Maine that summer—a place she and Dad loved to visit. Family friends were planning to take Mom to their time-share in Hawaii— because they knew that going to Hawaii was one of Mom's dreams.

To say that I was in a funk when I returned home after Mom's funeral is an understatement. I was in a place that was darker than any place I have ever been. My whole world had collapsed around me, and I felt adrift. I continued my trips back and forth to New York for another couple of months, to settle the estate, clean out my parents' house, and prepare it for sale. My physical and emotional exhaustion increased—and I knew I had to do something soon to pull myself out of this black hole.

For about a year prior to all this family trauma, I had been telling Jared that I needed to do something to combat the effects of age. Those pounds that suddenly appeared during the holidays were not disappearing as quickly as they used to. I was feeling a bit sluggish.

Jared—a lifelong runner—kept trying to get me to run with him. And I kept saying, "No, I'm not a runner. Can't do that. Maybe some other time." The real reason for my reluctance was that I didn't want to embarrass myself in front of my best friend. I mean, Jared had been running for years and could run rings around me. I couldn't run from here to there…or so I thought.

You see, growing up, I was about the least athletic kid you'd want to see. I was bad at every sport. And I was bullied because of my lack of athletic ability. I didn't want to risk subjecting myself to that kind of ridicule again, at age 57. (Remember earlier in the book when I said that one of the things that held me back from pursuing my show business dreams was the fear of being laughed at? Well, here I was again, in that same place!) But, Jared had planted the seed. And I knew that I needed to do something, because I was sinking further into the darkness.

I don't know what got into me, but in mid-April 2010— exactly one month after Mom's funeral—I contacted my friend,

Brett Malofsky, and asked him if he wanted to go for a run with me. We went out early one morning for an easy 1.5 mile jog. And I did it! And it felt kind of good! On our second or third run, Brett developed an injury and I lost my running buddy.

And then I sucked up my fears, and asked Jared if he would take me for a run. Jared pushed me a LOT harder than Brett had. For starters, Jared RAN from his house to my house for our first run together—about five miles round trip—talk about being intimidated!

We ran two miles that first time—including some little inclines. And Jared thought he was going to have to call the para-medics. I was wheezing, huffing, puffing, saying, "I can't do this." But I did make it back to my house on two feet. And that was the start of a new day for me—and my climb out of darkness.

Jared kept taking me out, encouraging me to run just a little further each week. I still marvel at how incredibly patient he was. How incredibly good I felt after each of those runs. How he got me to the point that I was ready to run my first 5K in September— just five months after I'd started. I finished that 5K race in just over 24 minutes. I did it!

This former wimpy kid had competed in his first-ever athletic event and did pretty well. It was at that moment of victory that I felt the missing piece of my life fall into place. For most of my life—probably due to the childhood bullying—I had felt "less than" because I did not do the things that the other guys did, and had no athletic talent. Now I felt whole.

I CAN do this! And that's when I started putting into practice what I preached to my clients—if you can think it, you can do it. If you believe in yourself, you can do it. Perhaps Henry Ford said it best—"Whether you think you can, or think you can't, either way you are right." I choose to think that I CAN.

Running became a life lesson for me—a metaphor for my life. For decades I had told myself that I was no good at sports. Couldn't compete. Was a loser. And sure enough, I wasn't any good at sports—because I told myself I wasn't any good. Yet, here I was, just a few months after taking my first, tentative run, competing in races.

After that first race in September, I entered a Turkey Trot Thanksgiving Day race in my town. Despite the fact that I tripped and fell, I picked myself back up, continued running—and finished that 5K in just over 23 minutes—shaving a full minute off my previous 5K time. In December, I ran the Deep Fried Turkey 5K—and finished in the Top 10!

Now it was time to get serious. Time to employ Jack Canfield's "Minimum, Target, Outrageous" system for achieving goals. My Minimum Goal was to run at least three days a week—and Jared held me accountable to that goal. My Target Goal was to run a 10K race—which I did on Cape Cod in February, 2011, finishing in just over 48 minutes.

My Outrageous Goal? To run a half marathon. In May, 2011, I ran the Cherry Tree Half Marathon in Rhode Island—and crossed the finish line in under two hours. A month later, I ran the Worcester (MA) Half Marathon. That October, I ran the Newport (RI) Half Marathon. Three half marathons in less than a year. How's that for achieving an Outrageous Goal?

I had achieved my Outrageous Goal—big time! Now what was I going to do? I needed a new goal. Oh, no…not a marathon. Me? Run 26.2 miles? Can't do it. Far beyond my ability. Jared convinced me otherwise, and in October 2012, we took a road trip to Atlantic City to run in the Atlantic City Marathon. There was a method to my madness. Atlantic City is flat. The marathon course is flat. If I was going to run 26.2 miles, it had to be FLAT! My goal was to finish in five hours.

I crossed the finish line in 4:48!

Shortly after returning home from Atlantic City, my friend Ken McDonnell, approached me about running in the 2013 Boston Marathon as a fundraiser for a non-profit he works for. Me? Run the Boston Marathon? You know, the one with Heartbreak Hill at

Mile 20? They don't call it Heartbreak Hill for nothing, you know. No—I'll never be able to run the Boston Marathon. Thanks for asking, though.

After a few weeks of thinking it over, I asked Jared if he thought I was capable of running the Boston Marathon. "Of course you can run Boston," he said, without a moment's hesitation. Jared had already accepted Ken's offer to join the Wake Up Narcolepsy team. So I got back in touch with Ken...only to find out that by that time, his organization had already filled their team. I was crestfallen. What was I going to do? Now I was desperate to get in—to prove to myself and to the world that I could do this.

Fortunately, my friend Ted Painter, who runs Boston every year, told me about some other organizations that field charity teams to run the Marathon—and the Boys and Girls Club of Newton (MA) invited me to join their Boston Marathon Team. This was another milestone for me—at age 59, the first time I had ever been asked to join an athletic team. (When I was a kid in school, I was always the last one picked for the team in gym class— no one wanted me!) And all I had to do to qualify was train—and agree to raise a minimum of $5000 for the Club.

What?

I'm not a fundraiser. How could I ask people to donate on behalf of my running? This was something entirely foreign to me. But I wanted to run the Boston Marathon—whatever it took to get there. I threw myself into my training and my fundraising. I became shameless about asking people for money. And asking again. And again. Soon, I discovered that people are willing to support you—all you have to do is ask. Someone donated $600 in my name. Another friend gave $500. Several more gave $100 each. Because they believed in my cause, and believed that I could accomplish my goal. Maybe they had more faith in my abilities than I did. I soon discovered that I was inspiring people by what I had accomplished with my running in such a short time and at my stage of life. And that's all I ever wanted in life—to inspire people, to make a difference in someone's life. Who knew that my dream would come true in the form of athletic competition?

We all know the tragedy that occurred at the finish line of the Boston Marathon on April 15, 2013. For me, it was eerily similar to what had happened in New York City on 9/11. I was less than a mile from the finish line when I was prevented from running any further. I didn't know exactly what was happening. Panic set in when I learned that bombs had gone off at the finish line. My first concern was Barbara. I had scored a VIP Pass for her to watch the race from the bleachers at the finish line. Was she there when the bombs went off? I didn't know where Jared—or his brother, Jason, who was also in the race—were, either—although I knew they were ahead of me. Were they near the finish line? Cell phone service had been blocked after the bombings—so I had no way to contact any of them. Fortunately, Barbara had been delayed by traffic, and was about 10 minutes away from the finish line when the bombs went off. And, as it turns out, Jared and Jason were less than 2/10 mile ahead of me when they were stopped. We were all safe.

Despite the tragedy of the day, I have nothing but good memories of running the Boston Marathon. It was my best, most joyful race to date. My friend Rachel, who was watching the race from the top of Heartbreak Hill, told me that I had a huge smile on my face as I powered up the hill. And, even though I didn't get to cross the finish line, I achieved something that day that I thought was far beyond my natural ability. Not only that, but according to Boston Athletic Association calculations, based on my running pace up to the point where I was stopped—I was on target to shave about five minutes off my Atlantic City Marathon time. WOW!!

I also witnessed so many glimmers of hope and healing in the hours after the marathon bombings. The runners who gathered around an older runner who was going into hypothermia, to keep him warm. The residents along Massachusetts Avenue who came out of their homes to offer us blankets and water. The woman who, when she saw me standing in a storefront, wearing nothing but my running shorts, singlet and running shoes as temperatures dropped—bedraggled-looking, caked in salt from sweating, and shivering as I waited to be reunited with Barbara—offered me her jacket to keep warm. After the senseless tragedy of the bombings, it restored my faith in the goodness of humankind.

Even better, though, was the fact that not only did I achieve my fundraising goal for the Boys and Girls Club—I exceeded it! Thanks to the generous support of over 100 family, friends and colleagues who believed in me, I raised $6500. This helped me to achieve yet another life goal—to be a philanthropist, and to be able to do something that makes a difference in the world. Just by running.

Running has transformed my life. It pulled me out of the depths of grief and despair. It brought me my best friend and business partner, Jared. It was while running that Jared and I came up with the concept for Mental Massage™. It was while running that we came up with the concept for this book.

Running has inspired me to push beyond my own, self-imposed limits. To continually test those limits. To live my life with vision, courage, determination and passion. And now, my success with running has, I am told, inspired and motivated others to reach beyond their own self-imposed limits, to live their lives with no limits.

Running allowed me to prove to myself that I CAN do ANYTHING I set my mind to—no matter the obstacles!

You never know where you will find your inspiration and your passion.

I AM a runner.

I AM an athlete.

I AM....

AND I AM GOING TO BE....

E P I L O G U E
Stop and Be Silent
Mary Wilson

Mary Wilson is a best-selling author, motivational speaker, actress, businesswoman, humanitarian, and former Cultural Ambassador for the United States Department of State. She is a founding member, along with Diana Ross and Florence Ballard, of the legendary Supremes—the most successful female vocal group in history. As the only member to remain with the group from their beginning in 1959 until they disbanded in 1977, Mary Wilson charted an incredible string of 12 Number One records, and over thirty Top Forty singles, selling in excess of 60 million copies. In show business for fifty-plus years, her solo career has continued to grow and evolve, now encompassing jazz and cabaret shows, as well as pop and rock concerts. Her 1986 autobiography, "Dreamgirl: My Life As A Supreme," was the most successful music biography of all time. She earned her Associate's Degree from New York University in 2001, and was awarded an honorary Doctorate of Humane Letters from Paine College, in Augusta, Georgia, in 2007.

Mary shares her personal philosophy of life:

I hope you have learned and benefitted from the life lessons shared in this book. The people profiled here have shared honestly with you about how they overcame specific obstacles in their lives in order to achieve their dreams. It's never easy living into your dreams. It's never easy. I know that first-hand. But life has been good to me!

There is so much wisdom all around us to guide us on our life's journey. What I would like to do is to share with you my philosophy of how I have handled obstacles when they have come into my life, without focusing on any one particular obstacle. Here's what I think….

I have moved through my life without allowing anything to really stop me. Now, that does not mean there have not been many, many situations in my life that have frightened or scared me. Honestly, though, I have never really looked at those situations as obstacles. I understand that, yes, life is always going to have its ups and downs. But I understand that when an obstacle gets in my way, I just have to find the way around it. I just wake up every morning, put my feet on the floor, start my day and keep moving. I have done that since I was a very young child. I have never really done anything more than simply keep moving forward.

My way of handling situations when they come up is to realize that I **can** do something about it right away; not do anything about it—or, wait until I figure out what's going on—and **then** make my decision about what to do. In other words, I just keep moving through it.

We all have that "fight or flight" instinct within us. It is what makes us do what we do—whether it's to run, or to stay and work it out. I have experienced it quite a few times in my life. The first time I remember it happening was when I was living in the Projects in Detroit. I was a very cute little girl, and I was always afraid that I would get jumped on, because that's what people did in those days if they thought you were weak or meek. I always had that fear as a child—and I wondered why it had never happened to me. No one ever beat me up. Then, one time, another girl actually chased me home. I knew that my choices were to either "fight or flee." I tried to run away from her, but she wouldn't give up. She just kept chasing me until finally she caught me and started beating me. Naturally, I started fighting back. That's how I am. I will try not to engage in certain things, because I might get hurt. But, I also have to protect myself.

As I look back on my life now, I realize that I have been given this great ability to patiently contemplate what initially I might not understand. I have been called a fence-sitter by quite a few people. When I was first told that, I wondered, "why would they say that about me?" You see, it is **not** that I **can't** make a decision. It's that I **choose** not to make a decision **until** I have **all the facts**. I think it is important to look into the situation before deciding, rather than being impetuous or doing just anything. I like to think things through. I am comfortable in waiting if I don't know what to do. And when I don't know what to do, I **choose** to do nothing. That has been a saving grace for me. I have seen a lot of people who just act on things because they feel they need to act—or someone else thinks they need to act **immediately**. And it has created problems for them.

You don't always have to act right away. Take the time to think through a situation before making your decision. I have this great ability to go inside myself, be silent, and see what I should do. When I get to the core knowledge about what I should do, then I work on it. Making decisions in this organic way really is very helpful.

For example, if we are playing a game and I don't understand all the rules, I won't play until I feel I understand the rules. I might still make mistakes, but at least I was operating from a position of knowing.

I never used to be able to put these things into words, but now I understand why I do what I do. Maybe you don't have all the answers right now. And that's OK. No one knows what is the best plan for you—**but you**. So take the time you need to figure it all out.

I see challenges in life—the challenges I have been through. But, I don't think of challenges as being negative. Those challenges have made me a stronger person. People say that I am a survivor, but I dislike that word. I don't think I am a survivor. I have moved through life from a position of certainty—of wanting to be sure. There have been, maybe, one or two situations that have set me back for a while. But I have never, ever, really stopped moving ahead. And, that is pretty profound, because I probably could be dead now had I acted in certain ways in certain situations. But, whenever I have been in a challenging situation, something has always saved me. Maybe it is because I think, and I feel. There have been times when I have been scared to death. But I never stopped moving. Maybe some people would call that survival. For me, it is just the way I have chosen to live my life.

My safeguard has always been to **stop** and be **silent**. We don't have enough silence in our lives. Throughout my life, I have what I call my "clicks and stops." I don't necessarily say, "OK, I am going to stop and meditate on that now." It just happens. All of a sudden, something will just "click," and I am not in control of my thoughts and my feelings. I am led to a place of quiet and calm, where I can stop and think. We all need to do this more. We just need to stop where we are, and go to that quiet spot for ourself.

It's like the Michael Jackson song, "Man in the Mirror." We don't often take the time to step back and really look at ourselves, and analyze where we are going in life. Maybe, because of some previous experience, we are afraid to go to that quiet place—afraid of what we might find there. Don't be afraid to really look at yourself honestly, and to listen to that "still, small voice" inside of you. You will find your answers within yourself.

That is my way. To be still. To go inside myself. I have always loved being by myself, being quiet. I am Pisces, though—the fish swimming in both directions! So, while I truly love being on stage, and going out with people, that is not 100% who I am. I also love being alone.

So here is what I want to say to those of you who may be feeling that life itself is an insurmountable obstacle. Just stop, and be still. As they say, after the storm comes the rainbow. I know that to be true. If you can just make it through the night, things may not seem so bleak in the morning. In the light of day, you can get over that "fright" mode, think more clearly, and make a move. That is so much better than making a quick decision that you will regret later. I love the song, Smile," written by Charlie Chaplin— "you'll find the sun comes shining through for you…if you just smile." It's true—it really does work!

Teach the children in your life the importance of being silent. If we nurture that skill early in life, you will have a way of solving problems and finding the answers that will last a lifetime. It is worth the work to start asking the questions, so that the answers will come.

Life is pretty vast—but it is also pretty simple, when you really think about it.

There is a great quote by poet SJ Kalinich that I have posted on my website that I would like to share with you:

"Slow down, stand guard, porter, at the windows of your consciousness. Only let peaceful good people in. Dismiss the rest with grace and kindness."

Look honestly at yourself and ask the questions. Then slow down and listen. The answers will come.

And never, ever give up your dreams. Never let anyone tell you that your dreams are silly or unimportant. Know your worth as an individual—and never let anyone take that from you. Dare to dream—and to dream big dreams.

And when you achieve your dreams, I want you to dream again, and again, and again….

PART TWO

Living Into My Dreams
My Personal Dream Journal

My Personal Dream Journal

We hope you have been inspired by the personal stories shared in Part One of this book. Each of the individuals profiled has shared with you openly and honestly about their journey, and shared with you the lessons they have learned along the way. Now it is time for you to take the pearls of wisdom shared by our guides, and apply them to your own life. This is YOUR opportunity to develop the road map to get from where you are now to where you want to be in life...with vision, courage, determination and passion. Full speed ahead, emergency brake off—speed bumps and all!

When is the last time you took the time to step back from the hustle and bustle of your daily life to really focus on your own goals and dreams, hopes and aspirations, values, interests, road-blocks, and fears? The following pages contain a series of systematic self-assessment tools designed to help you take 100% responsibility for your life, to identify your true passion, and discover how to live into YOUR dreams. These assessments will help you to clarify and set your goals, and then develop the plan to ACHIEVE your goals. These self-assessment tools—and the self-motivational tips and techniques we share—will, we hope, help you to enhance your sense of worth as an individual, and to tap into the power you already have within you to achieve your goals—no matter the obstacles!

Also included here are some journal pages so that you can record your thoughts and feelings as you continue on your journey into your best life. Remember—it is not the destination we reach that is the most rewarding. It is the journey itself. Record your thoughts and feelings as you journey, and when you reach the top of the mountain—and you will, we KNOW you will!—think of all of the people in this book who guided you along the path. You are in very good company!

The assessment tools in this section of the book are not designed to be psychological tests, nor should they be construed as such. They are intended simply to provide you with clues and building blocks as you formulate your personal plan to live into your dreams.

Some of the assessment tools and self-motivational tips are influenced by and based on the work of Jack Canfield's *The Success Principles: How to Get From Where You Are to Where You Want to Be*. New York: HarperCollins, 2005. www.thesuccessprinciples.com

Are you ready? Then let's take that first step…it's always the hardest….

> "Faith is taking the first step, even when
> you don't see the whole staircase."
> **MARTIN LUTHER KING, JR.**

My Life and Where I Want To Be in Five Years

Answer each of the following questions on a scale of 1 to 3, with 1 indicating that you have a high degree of clarity on your purpose in life, and 3 indicating that you do not know yourself or your life purpose as well as you would like. The lower your score, the better you are at knowing what you want and how to get it. A higher score indicates that you need to do some more work to clarify and set your goals.

_____ 1. I can easily list my Top Four life goals.

_____ 2. I know what I want and where I want to be in five years.

_____ 3. I can describe my life goals to others easily in a 60-second "elevator pitch."

_____ 4. I have developed my own, personal mission statement for my life, which determines which activities I will pursue to accomplish my goals.

_____ 5. I know what is important to me.

_____ 6. I am self-assured and have a good sense of my skills and my abilities.

_____ 7. I can easily list my Top Four personal qualities.

_____ 8. If someone asks me, "What do you want in life," I can answer without hesitation.

_____ 9. I am certain of my values, priorities, hopes and dreams.

_____ 10. I am not averse to taking risks in order to get what I want in life.

_____ 11. When making decisions, I am able to assess the long-term implications of that decision on my life plan.

_____ 12. I have a clearly articulated life plan that encompasses all aspects of my life (personal, professional, financial, health).

_____ 13. I am comfortable meeting new people and can articulate who I am to them.

_____ 14. I am clear about what motivates me to achieve my dreams.

_____ 15. I am the person I want to be and am on track to get where I want to be in five years.

ᘐ

Self-Motivational Tip

It's OK to daydream!

Meditation or guided visualization is a great way to achieve greater clarity of who you are, what you want—and how to get there. As you meditate and relax your mind, your subconscious mind will begin to give you images of the things that are important to you—your hopes and dreams, goals and aspirations—some of which may have been buried there for years! Use these mental clues to form the basis of your life plan. Do it often—the more you visualize, the greater clarity you will achieve!

Assess Your Skills

1. The three activities I am so passionate about that I can't wait to jump out of bed in the morning are:

A. _____

B. _____

C. _____

2. What skills do I need in my personal toolbox to be successful in these three activities?

A. _____

B. _____

C. _____

D. _____

3. What strengths do I bring to the table?

A. _____

B. _____

C. _____

D. _____

4. What areas do I need to work on?

A. _____

B. _____

C. _____

D. _____

∾

Self-Motivational Tip

Take time EVERY day to visualize yourself in your dream life or dream career. The thoughts and images that you put into your head are the things that will begin to manifest in your life. Remember, you are what you think!

How Motivated Am I To Achieve?

Achieving your goals requires courage and risk. We know that first-hand. In order to succeed, you need to be able to motivate yourself, rather than relying on others to define your goals and dreams. This assessment will help you to determine how strong your internal drive is to achieve your dream.

Rate each statement on a scale of 1 to 3, with 1 indicating, "I have a strong drive to achieve my dreams," and 3 indicating, "I am more comfortable with someone else motivating me to achieve my goals." A lower score indicates that you are likely to strive for excellence, and that goal achievement is your primary motivator. A higher score may indicate that you look to others for direction and motivation.

_____ 1. I feel good when I think about my future and my dreams.

_____ 2. Rather than striving for perfection, I derive my satisfaction from knowing that I did my best.

_____ 3. My own sense of accomplishment is more important than receiving praise from others for my efforts.

_____ 4. I have the ability to initiate, execute and complete a project on my own, with no outside direction.

_____ 5. I am willing to take risks and consider new options in order to achieve my dreams.

_____ 6. Rather than viewing difficult situations as obstacles or problems, I look at them as opportunities and challenges.

_____ 7. I am able to establish, and stick to, my own deadlines for accomplishing a goal.

_____ 8. I am motivated by my own definition of success, rather than by external rewards or praise.

_____ 9. Throughout my life, I have been a high-achiever.

_____ 10. I am good at solving problems with little or no outside-prompting.

_____ 11. I can clearly articulate my goals, and then develop the action plan to achieve them.

_____ 12. My colleagues and friends often tell me that they are inspired by my drive to achieve my goals.

_____ 13. When a plan I try does not produce the desired results, I do not give up. I try something new.

_____ 14. I approach new projects with a sense of enthusiasm and a "can-do" attitude. I KNOW I will accomplish my goal.

_____ 15. I am a self-starter, and can easily motivate myself to achieve a new goal.

Self-Motivational Tip

You are the only one who knows what is best for you. Don't allow someone else to define your dreams or goals for you. If there is something you have always wanted to do—DO IT!! At least give it a try. You can only regret the chances you don't take! Step out on faith—what some people refer to as "deep water faith."

Ask Yourself this question

What do I want to do right now, so that I do not regret NOT doing it twenty years from now?

How Well Do I Manage Stress?

With the hustle and bustle of daily life, we all experience stress. Stress is not necessarily a bad thing. It doesn't mean there is something wrong with you. The key factor is whether you are able to manage your stress—or if you let stress manage you. This assessment will help you to determine how well you manage the stress in your life.

Assess each statement on a scale of 1 to 3—with 1 being, "I am able to manage stress well," and 3 being, "I am not coping well with the stress in my life." A lower score indicates that you have good stress management strategies in place. A higher score indicates that you may be letting your stress manage you.

_____ 1. I am always saying how stressed out I am.

_____ 2. There are many days when I feel overwhelmed.

_____ 3. When I feel overwhelmed or stressed out, I tend to "shut down" both physically and emotionally.

_____ 4. My friends and family tell me that I need to relax more.

_____ 5. When I am overwhelmed, I am irritable and impatient.

_____ 6. When I am stressed out, I tend to turn to food and alcohol to help me relax.

_____ 7. I typically put off dealing with difficult situations, rather than addressing them immediately.

_____ 8. I often think that I do not possess good problem-solving or stress management skills.

_____ 9. There are many days when I don't know how to accomplish all that is on my plate.

_____ 10. I do not take time on a regular basis to participate in activities that I enjoy or that calm me.

_____ 11. When I begin to feel stressed out, my shoulders tense and I get a headache.

_____ 12. I am not good at prioritizing my daily "to do" list—everything seems like a priority.

_____ 13. I do not ask others for help when I feel stressed out by a task because I do not want them to know that I am overwhelmed.

_____ 14. When I start to feel stressed out, I try to take steps to deal with it immediately.

_____ 15. I think I deal well with the stress in my life, even when something unexpected happens.

∽

Self-Motivational Tip

Take time every day to do something that is soul satisfying to you—something that nourishes your soul, brings you joy, and helps calm you. It may be meditating, or reading, or gardening, or taking a walk, or listening to music—whatever works best for you. Even if you have only fifteen minutes, do this EVERY day. When you are calm and relaxed, you are better able to achieve a greater degree of clarity about how to accomplish your goals.

"Whether you think you can, or think you can't,
either way you're right."
Henry Ford

The Person I Was Born to Be (My Purpose for Being)

The personal qualities that I believe make me unique are:

_____

_____

_____

_____

I demonstrate these qualities by:

_____

_____

_____

_____

My world would be perfect if:

_____

_____

_____

_____

My unique qualities can benefit my perfect world in the following ways:

_____

_____

_____

_____

Based on your responses to the above, write what will serve as your personal mission statement. My mission in life is to:

_____

_____

_____

_____

We know that most businesses have mission statements—guiding principles that define their reason for being. It is just as important for us, as individuals, to have a personal statement—that defines our reason for being, and helps us to determine what activities to pursue, and how to pursue them.

Once you have crafted your own, personal mission statement, review it often. This will guide you as you clarify your dreams and set your goals.

"To know oneself, one should assert oneself."
ALBERT CAMUS

What Are The Steps To My Dream?

Now is the time for me to start living into my dreams—beginning today!

1. Ever since I can remember, my dream has been to:

    _____

2. Today,_____, I will take Step One in developing my personal road map to achieve my dreams.

3. I plan to achieve the following four goals during the next twelve months:
    A. _____
    B. _____
    C. _____
    D. _____

4. In order to achieve my goals, I need to overcome the following obstacles—real or imagined—in my life:
    A. _____
    B. _____
    C. _____
    D. _____

5. In order to triumph over my personal obstacles, I plan to:
    A. _____
    B. _____
    C. _____
    D. _____

6. To help me stay on track with my plan and hold me accountable, I will ask_____ (name of a trusted friend or family member) to check in with me every two weeks and assess my progress. This person will serve as my personal success coach.

7. I make this commitment to myself in order to live into my dreams—to live my life without limits!

_____
(name & date)

Self-Motivational Tip

Is fear one of your obstacles? Remember, many times, fear is **False Evidence Appearing Real** (F.E.A.R.).

Establishing My Vision for My Life

Throughout my life, the dream or goal that I have been most passionate about is:

_____

_____

_____

_____

This dream has held my attention over time because:

_____

_____

_____

_____

In order to make my dream come true, I need to:

_____

_____

_____

_____

By pursuing my dream, I can make a difference in the world by:

_____

_____

_____

_____

When I daydream or visualize, my perfect life includes:

_____

_____

_____

_____

Twenty years from now, I will know that I am successful if I have accomplished:

_____

_____

_____

_____

The best use of my time, talents, creativity and vision is to:

_____

_____

_____

_____

"Imagination is the beginning of creation.
You imagine what you desire; you will what you imagine;
and at last you create what you will."
GEORGE BERNARD SHAW

Mind-Mapping

Mind-mapping is an easy—yet powerful—way to create a visual "to-do" list for achieving your dreams. Your mind-map lets you determine what information you need to gather, what you need to do, whom you need to consult, the steps you need to take, how much money you need, your deadlines, etc.—for each of your dreams.

To create your Mind-Map for your dreams, follow these steps:

1. Draw a circle in the center of a piece of paper. Write the name of your dream in the center of the circle.

2. Draw a larger circle around your center circle. Divide this larger circle into segments representing the major categories of tasks you will need to accomplish in order to achieve your dream.

3. Draw spokes radiating outward from each segment of your outer circle. Label each spoke with each step you need to take. Then, break down each step into more detailed action items, from which you will create your "to-do" list.

When you have finished mind-mapping your dream, convert all of your action items into a daily "to-do" list. Commit to a completion date for each item. Put it on your calendar—and be sure to do something every day to stay on course!

∾

Self-Motivational Tip
Write It Down!

Writing down your dream(s), action items, and deadlines on paper provides a powerful visual motivation to keep you on track. Once it is committed to paper, it's real. And once you commit to a deadline—in writing—you don't want to let yourself down, do you? In fact, some people like to jot their dream on a sticky note and post it on their bathroom mirror—so that it is the first thing they see every morning! That way, you won't forget about your goal.

Am I Living My Life "On Purpose"?

This assessment will help you to determine if you are focused on achieving your dreams and goals.

Rate each statement on a scale of 1 to 3, with 1 being, "I am focused on my dream," and 3 being, "I need to re-focus in order to achieve my dream." The lower your score, the more strategically focused you are on achieving your dreams and goals.

_____ 1. I know what my purpose in life is.

_____ 2. I make decisions easily and am able to follow through on my decisions.

_____ 3. I am able to avoid distractions that may sidetrack my attention.

_____ 4. I am good at seeing the Big Picture and how all the pieces will fit together.

_____ 5. I like to have a plan in place to avoid making impetuous decisions.

_____ 6. I have so many interests that it is difficult for me to set priorities. Everything is important.

_____ 7. When I have a new idea for my life, I am able to think it through and create a plan to accomplish it.

_____ 8. I am able to clearly see the best direction for my life.

_____ 9. People often say they admire my ability to pursue my goals with determination and commitment.

_____ 10. I approach my decision-making in a calm and centered way.

_____ 11. I know how much I can handle and do not let myself get overwhelmed by biting off more than I can chew.

_____ 12. I am able to maintain my enthusiasm and energy level until I have accomplished my task.

_____ 13. My colleagues look to me for leadership because I am able to clearly articulate a goal and then set a plan to achieve it.

_____ 14. When called upon to do so, I am able to multi-task by setting priorities.

_____ 15. I am able to see the opportunities in any situation.

Pulling It All Together—My Personal Road Map for Success!

By now, you have read everyone's stories of how they overcame the obstacles in their lives to achieve their goals. We have shared our accumulated wisdom with you. You have completed nine other Self-Assessments. Now, it is time to put everything you have learned together into your personal road map to success. **NOW** is the time to make a commitment to yourself to live into **YOUR** dreams. To live **YOUR** life with **NO** limits. To achieve **YOUR FULL** potential. You have fifteen guides to help you along your journey.

By committing **IN WRITING** to work on the following five areas of your life—**AND** committing to a firm deadline by which you will achieve your goals—you are taking that **ONE GIANT STEP** into your bright, new future. You have the road map. There are **NO** excuses now. Take the emergency brake off. Full speed ahead into the life of your dreams!

1. The areas of my life that I need to work on in order to improve myself are:

   A. _____

   B. _____

   C. _____

2. The three things that serve to distract me from my goal, and that I can spend LESS time on are:

   A. _____

   B. _____

   C. _____

3. The three things that ARE working well in my life, that are moving me in the direction of my goal, and that I can spend MORE time doing are:

A. _____

B. _____

C. _____

4. Three strategies I have not yet tried, but which may move me in the direction of my goal are:

A. _____

B. _____

C. _____

5. As a result of reading this book, and completing the Self-Assessments, I make a commitment to myself to do the following:

A. _____

B. _____

C. _____

6. I commit to myself to accomplish this by the following date:

A. _____

B. _____

C. _____

Affirmations

Affirmations are a powerful tool for placing positive thoughts into your conscious and subconscious thoughts. They affirm your own goodness, and the power you already have within to achieve anything you put your mind to. Make affirmations a part of your daily habit—during your meditation time, while running, when you first wake up in the morning or right before you go to sleep at night. Whatever works best for you. Put it out to the Universe; the Universe will give you exactly what you ask for. Here are some sample affirmations to get you started—but create affirmations for yourself that are meaningful to you on a deep personal level:

I believe in God

I believe in people

I believe in me

I am asking to be open to a life of YES

I believe that I can be open to a life of YES

I am receiving a life of YES

I am asking to (whatever your goal is)

I believe that I am currently (whatever progress you are making toward your goal)

I am receiving (whatever you need to help you achieve your goal; for example: leads, referrals, money) from (your goal)

I am grateful for (your goal)

I am asking to release and let it go

I believe that I can release and let it go

I believe that I am releasing and letting it go

I believe that I have released and let it go

I am receiving peace, love and joy because I have released and let it go

I am grateful for peace, love and joy from releasing and letting it go

I am thankful for God

I am thankful for the people in my life

I am thankful for me

Special thanks to Scott Lamlein, of North Forty Road Web Design and North Forty Road Music, for sharing these affirmations with us. Scott's CD of piano music for meditation and relaxation, "Peace," is perfect for personal meditation, relaxation, and music therapy. The simple, accessible melodies invoke a quiet that calms the soul. "Peace" is available for download from iTunes and Amazon, as well as from Scott's website (www.nfrmusic.com). We use Scott's CD during the guided visualization portion of all our Mental Massage® workshops.

Self-Motivational Tips and Techniques

Here are some of our favorite self-motivational tips and techniques. Use these as a guide to keep you on track as you move closer to your goal every day:

Tip #1: We are firm believers in Jack Canfield's **"The Success Principles,"** In his books and seminars, Canfield suggests establishing what he calls a **"Breakthrough Goal"** for yourself—something that represents one giant step forward in your life—whether personal or professional. This gives you something to focus on and to aim for. It is that thing that will just knock your socks off when you achieve it.

Tip #2: Canfield further provides what we feel is a foolproof method for setting and achieving your goal—**"MTO—Minimum-Target-Outrageous."** Canfield suggests that whenever you set a goal, you first set your **Minimum Goal**—something that you know you can achieve. Reaching that goal will, in turn, keep you motivated to move toward your **Target Goal**—which will require you to stretch just a little farther to achieve. Your **Outrageous Goal**? That is your ultimate goal—the thing that when you achieve it, you will say, "WOW—I never dreamed I could do THAT!" Refer to Chapter 15 to find out how Tom set his MTO Goals for running.

Tip #3: Practice this mantra every day: **"Progress, not perfection."** You don't have to do it perfectly the first time. But you DO have to get it going! Don't let striving for perfection block your progress toward reaching your goal. It is OK to make mistakes—as long as you learn from them, pick yourself up, and continue moving in the direction of your goal. Strive for excellence, not perfection.

Tip #4: Recent research indicates that there is a link between meditation and brain function. People who meditate are better able to regulate their emotional responses to situations, and are more compassionate—making them better able to assist others in need. Even though meditation is a solitary activity, it can have an impact on your family, neighborhood, community, and the world at large. Meditate every day!

Tip #5: Related to the above, take time for yourself every day. Do something that is soul satisfying—something that is meaningful to you, whether it be gardening, reading, meditating, etc. Nurture and nourish your soul. You will find that you are more open to the messages and clues that the Universe is sending you.

Tip #6: Never let anyone take your sense of self-worth away from you. Keep believing in yourself. You **ARE** a person of worth!

Tip #7: Know what strengths you bring to the table—and don't be afraid to tell others what they are.

Tip #8: Don't ever let anyone—especially yourself—tell you that your dreams are silly, unimportant, or unattainable. Dreams are your subconscious mind's way of telling you what you really want. No one knows what is best for you but YOU!

Tip #9: We are continually faced with amazing opportunities that present themselves as unsolvable problems. We both know that first-hand. Opportunities may not always be perfect. But if you don't take them when they are offered, they may never come again. Once you know what you want—what you **REALLY** want— in life, you are better able to recognize the opportunities that are right in front of you every day. Seize those imperfect opportunities that are presented to you and make them your own.

Tip #10: When you are standing at the edge of your dreams, you can walk away—or you can soar. The choice is yours—give it all you've got and choose to soar!

Tip #11: Don't wait for Prince or Princess Charming to come along and make the slipper fit. Don't wait for someone else to make your dreams come true. Yes—accept the helping hand when it is offered to you, just as we both did. But YOU are ultimately responsible for your own happiness. YOU have the power within yourself to achieve your heart's desires. It's already there. Go out and win your life—expect to win.

Tip #12: Learn from the turtle. It only makes progress when it sticks its neck out. Living life successfully and achieving your dreams requires great courage and risk.

Tip #13: Gather together a small group of friends or colleagues whom you trust implicitly to be brutally honest with you. Jack Canfield calls it a **"Mastermind Group."** Others call it an **"Accountability Group."** Use this group as a sounding board as you develop your road map to get from where you are to where you want to be in life. This provides two critical benefits. First, once you share your dreams or goals with others, they are out there, you have committed to them, and it will be harder for you to slack off. Your Accountability Group will do just that—hold you accountable and keep you on track as you move closer to your goal. They will hold your feet to the fire. And they will help you determine if you are on the right path, moving in the right direction. It is essential that you trust this group to be brutally honest—and that you can accept their honesty.

Tip #14: A great way to make sure that you stay satisfied and productive—whether in your personal life or professional life—is to check in with yourself periodically to identify what you are most passionate about in life. Identifying and understanding your true passions in life will help to guide you in your journey.

Tip #15: Face your challenges head-on. Don't give up when the going gets tough, or when things don't work out exactly as you planned. Who knows—there just may be a bigger plan for you!

Some of Our Favorite Inspirational Quotes and Sayings

"I dream my painting, then I paint my dream."
VINCENT VAN GOGH

"In the long run, we shape our lives and we shape ourselves."
ELEANOR ROOSEVELT

"Imagination is everything.
It is the preview of life's coming attractions"
ALBERT EINSTEIN

"All that we are is a result of all we have thought."
BUDDHA

"Whether you think that you can or think you can't,
either way you're right."
HENRY FORD

"When you turn your dream into fact, you are in
a position to build bigger and bigger dreams.
And that is…the creative process."
BOB PROCTOR

"There is no dream that may not come true, if you but
learn to use the creative force working through you…
the key…lies in using what you have."
ROBERT COLLIER

"How does one become a butterfly?
You must want to fly so much that you are willing to
give up being a caterpillar."
TRINA PAULUS

"You can have anything you want if you are willing to give up
the belief that you can't have it."
ROBERT ANTHONY

"In order to be effective, truth must penetrate like an arrow—
and that is likely to hurt."
WEI WU WEI

"The dreamers are the saviors of the world."
JAMES ALLEN

"Don't ask what the world needs. Ask what makes
you come alive, and go do it. Because what the world needs is
people who have come alive."
HOWARD THURMAN

"The creation of a thousand forests is in one acorn."
RALPH WALDO EMERSON

"Worry a little bit every day and in a lifetime you will lose a
couple of years. If something is wrong, fix it if you can. But train
yourself not to worry. Worry never fixes anything."
MARY HEMINGWAY

"Here is the test to find whether your mission on Earth is finished: if you're alive, it isn't."
RICHARD BACH

"Imagination is the beginning of creation.
You imagine what you desire; you will want what you imagine;
and at last you create what you will."
GEORGE BERNARD SHAW

"Raise your sail one foot and you gain ten feet of wind."
CHINESE PROVERB

"Our life always expresses the result of our dominant thoughts."
SOREN KIERKEGAARD

"I don't think of all the misery, but of the beauty that still remains. My advice is: Go outside, to the fields, enjoy nature and the sunshine, go out and try to recapture happiness in yourself and in God. Think of all the beauty that is still left in and around you and be happy!"
ANNE FRANK

"Decision is a risk rooted in the courage of being free."
PAUL TILLICH

"Don't try to be better than your contemporaries or predecessors. Try to be better than yourself."
WILLIAM FAULKNER

"Success is to be measured not so much by the position that one has reached in life as by the obstacles which he has overcome while trying to succeed."
BOOKER T. WASHINGTON

"Use the talents you possess, for the woods would be a very silent place if no birds sang except the best."
HENRY VAN DYKE

"Know the limits in everything and you will never know the passion."
LEONID SUKHORUKOV

"The greatest pleasure in life is doing the things people say we cannot do."
WALTER BAGEHOT

Dreams come true through hard work.

Dreams come true through dedication.

Dreams come true by staying focused on your goal.

Have the courage to change.

Seize opportunities.

My Personal Dream Diary

Use the following pages to keep track of the steps you have taken toward achieving your dreams and goals, what you have learned about yourself in the process, and what you have accomplished...

TODAY'S DATE

MY GOAL

MY PLAN

IN THE PROCESS, I LEARNED

HOW DO I FEEL ABOUT WHAT I ACCOMPLISHED?

THE NEXT STEP I NEED TO TAKE IS

MY PERSONAL DREAM JOURNAL

TODAY'S DATE

MY GOAL

MY PLAN

IN THE PROCESS, I LEARNED

HOW DO I FEEL ABOUT WHAT I ACCOMPLISHED?

THE NEXT STEP I NEED TO TAKE IS

Today's Date

My Goal

My Plan

In The Process, I Learned

How Do I Feel About What I Accomplished?

The Next Step I Need To Take Is

TODAY'S DATE

My Goal

My Plan

In The Process, I Learned

How Do I Feel About What I Accomplished?

The Next Step I Need To Take Is

TODAY'S DATE

MY GOAL

MY PLAN

IN THE PROCESS, I LEARNED

HOW DO I FEEL ABOUT WHAT I ACCOMPLISHED?

THE NEXT STEP I NEED TO TAKE IS

My Personal Dream Journal

TODAY'S DATE

My Goal

My Plan

In The Process, I Learned

How Do I Feel About What I Accomplished?

The Next Step I Need To Take Is

Today's Date

My Goal

My Plan

In The Process, I Learned

How Do I Feel About What I Accomplished?

The Next Step I Need To Take Is

TODAY'S DATE

MY GOAL

MY PLAN

IN THE PROCESS, I LEARNED

HOW DO I FEEL ABOUT WHAT I ACCOMPLISHED?

THE NEXT STEP I NEED TO TAKE IS

TODAY'S DATE

My Goal

My Plan

In The Process, I Learned

How Do I Feel About What I Accomplished?

The Next Step I Need To Take Is

TODAY'S DATE

MY GOAL

MY PLAN

IN THE PROCESS, I LEARNED

HOW DO I FEEL ABOUT WHAT I ACCOMPLISHED?

THE NEXT STEP I NEED TO TAKE IS

TODAY'S DATE

MY GOAL

MY PLAN

IN THE PROCESS, I LEARNED

HOW DO I FEEL ABOUT WHAT I ACCOMPLISHED?

THE NEXT STEP I NEED TO TAKE IS

TODAY'S DATE

MY GOAL

MY PLAN

IN THE PROCESS, I LEARNED

HOW DO I FEEL ABOUT WHAT I ACCOMPLISHED?

THE NEXT STEP I NEED TO TAKE IS

TODAY'S DATE

MY GOAL

MY PLAN

IN THE PROCESS, I LEARNED

HOW DO I FEEL ABOUT WHAT I ACCOMPLISHED?

THE NEXT STEP I NEED TO TAKE IS

My Personal Dream Journal

TODAY'S DATE

My Goal

My Plan

In The Process, I Learned

How Do I Feel About What I Accomplished?

The Next Step I Need To Take Is

One Door Closes

My Personal Dream Journal

TODAY'S DATE

My Goal

My Plan

In The Process, I Learned

How Do I Feel About What I Accomplished?

The Next Step I Need To Take Is

TODAY'S DATE

MY GOAL

MY PLAN

IN THE PROCESS, I LEARNED

HOW DO I FEEL ABOUT WHAT I ACCOMPLISHED?

THE NEXT STEP I NEED TO TAKE IS

TODAY'S DATE

My Goal

My Plan

In The Process, I Learned

How Do I Feel About What I Accomplished?

The Next Step I Need To Take Is

TODAY'S DATE

MY GOAL

MY PLAN

IN THE PROCESS, I LEARNED

HOW DO I FEEL ABOUT WHAT I ACCOMPLISHED?

THE NEXT STEP I NEED TO TAKE IS

TODAY'S DATE

MY GOAL

MY PLAN

IN THE PROCESS, I LEARNED

HOW DO I FEEL ABOUT WHAT I ACCOMPLISHED?

THE NEXT STEP I NEED TO TAKE IS

Today's Date

My Goal

My Plan

In The Process, I Learned

How Do I Feel About What I Accomplished?

The Next Step I Need To Take Is

MY PERSONAL DREAM JOURNAL

TODAY'S DATE

MY GOAL

MY PLAN

IN THE PROCESS, I LEARNED

HOW DO I FEEL ABOUT WHAT I ACCOMPLISHED?

THE NEXT STEP I NEED TO TAKE IS

Today's Date

My Goal

My Plan

In The Process, I Learned

How Do I Feel About What I Accomplished?

The Next Step I Need To Take Is

MY PERSONAL DREAM JOURNAL

TODAY'S DATE

MY GOAL

MY PLAN

IN THE PROCESS, I LEARNED

HOW DO I FEEL ABOUT WHAT I ACCOMPLISHED?

THE NEXT STEP I NEED TO TAKE IS

Today's Date

My Goal

My Plan

In The Process, I Learned

How Do I Feel About What I Accomplished?

The Next Step I Need To Take Is

TODAY'S DATE

My Goal

My Plan

In The Process, I Learned

How Do I Feel About What I Accomplished?

The Next Step I Need To Take Is

MY PERSONAL DREAM JOURNAL

TODAY'S DATE

MY GOAL

MY PLAN

IN THE PROCESS, I LEARNED

HOW DO I FEEL ABOUT WHAT I ACCOMPLISHED?

THE NEXT STEP I NEED TO TAKE IS

Resources

The MotivAct Group LLC offers a full portfolio of holistic personal and professional development workshops and seminars designed to help you clarify, set and achieve your goals, reduce stress, and enhance your mind/body balance.

Our signature program is **Mental Massage**™ —an innovative fusion of guided visualization and re-energizing massage in a transformational group workshop. Other programs include:

Strategies to Achieve Your Goals and Manage Stress

Making A Difference Begins With YOU…So Live Into Your Dreams!

Strategies to Manage Stress for Caregivers

Visioning for Non-Profit Boards

10 Things Every Business Should Know About Copyright

Individual Coaching for Success

To find out more about bringing one of our programs to your organization, or to schedule individual coaching, please visit our website, and use the Contact Page:

www.motivactgroup.com

TO LEARN MORE ABOUT THE PEOPLE AND
ORGANIZATIONS PROFILED IN THIS BOOK, PLEASE VISIT
THEIR WEBSITES (where available):

Tom Ingrassia: www.ingrassiaproductions.com

Jared Chrudimsky: www.revitalizetherapy.com

Mary Wilson: www.marywilson.com

Scherrie Payne: www.scherriepayneandlyndalaurence.com

Scott Erb & Donna Dufault: www.erbphotography.com

Annette Rafferty/Abby's House: www.abbyshouse.org

Corrie Painter/Angiosarcoma Awareness, Inc.:
www.cureasc.org

Ken McDonnell/Wake Up Narcolepsy:
www.wakeupnarcolepsy.org

**Rev. Shandarai Mawokomatanda/Wesley United Methodist
Church:** www.wesleyworc.org

January Jones: www.januaryjones.com

Nancy Dube: www.dubeconsulting.com

Reed Nixon: www.sherylnixon.com

Glenn Nazarian:
www.facebook.com/pages/Boston-North-Fitness

(**NOTE:** Mary Wilson, Annette Rafferty, January Jones, and Reed Nixon have their own books, which you may wish to read to learn more about their lives.)

ALSO SEE:

Canfield, Jack. *The Success Principles: How To Get From Where You Are to Where You Want to Be*, HarperCollins, 2005. www.thesuccessprinciples.com

"Peace" meditation CD, composed and performed by Scott Lamlein. www.nfrmusic.com

CPSIA information can be obtained
at www.ICGtesting.com
Printed in the USA
FFOW05n2239110614

9 781939 288257